SMALL
RADIO
CONTROL
BOATS

GLYNN GUEST

Special Interest Model Books

Special Interest Model Books Ltd.
P.O.Box 327
Poole
Dorset
BH15 2RG
England

First published by Argus Books Ltd. 1998
This edition published by Special Interest Model Books Ltd. 2005

ISBN 1-85486-171-9

www.specialinterstmodelbooks.co.uk

Printed and bound in Great Britain by CPI Bath

CONTENTS

INTRODUCTION

Models operated using radio control equipment have developed tremendously in the past couple of decades. Perhaps the greatest change has occurred with the availability of reliable and easy to use commercial radio control outfits. The price of these outfits has fallen dramatically in real terms and the actual construction of the models can now be the most expensive part of the hobby.

The time and cost of building a new model can be reduced by taking advantage of the small size of radio control equipment. It is quite practical to build a model boat down to a length of no more than 38cm (15 inches) which can accommodate the R/C gear, motors and batteries, yet still be a safe and reliable performer. Another bonus is that such small models encourage you to try new and novel ideas that might not be worth risking in a larger and hence more expensive model.

Most of the plans that follow have been published in the magazine *Model Boats*. Indeed the editor was responsible for my first attempt at small R/C models when he asked if I had ever tried to build something that would fit across a double page spread of his magazine. There is no reason why you cannot change the designs to suit your own needs or tastes. As most of the parts have simple shapes, it ought to be easy to enlarge a plan if you need something bigger. Be warned though, if you double the model's size then its weight is increased eight-fold!

General notes

All of the models described make use of balsawood and card in their construction. Likewise, for economy and ease of control, electric motors power these models. Rather than repeat the same comments with each model, some general notes on construction and outfitting are given first.

Basic terms

One possible source of confusion is that different modellers can use different names for the same features and parts. I will try to be consistent and use the following terms.

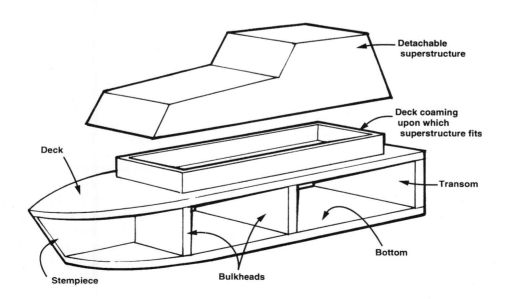

Detachable superstructure

Deck coaming upon which superstructure fits

Deck

Transom

Stempiece

Bulkheads

Bottom

Balsawood

This is a convenient material to use as it is available in a wide range of sheet and strip sizes from most model shops. It's easy to cut and shape nature is complemented by more than adequate strength for models such as these.

If you look through a model shop's selection of balsa then it ought to become apparent that balsa can come in a wide range of density and strength. The softest grades can be prone to damage while the hard grades can be very difficult to cut and work with. The best grade to use is a medium one somewhere between these two extremes.

One feature to avoid is an uneven grain pattern in the balsa. This can make cutting parts out more difficult and possibly weaken the final model. A uniform straight grain pattern is ideal with no obvious changes in density or stiffness.

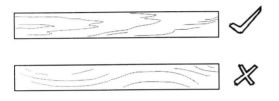

Something else to check is that the balsa sheets and strips are straight and square edged. No twists or bends should be visible when viewed along the length of the balsa.

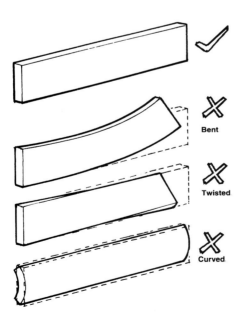

Luckily balsawood suppliers take great care to ensure that only a good quality and uniform product ends up in a model shop's stock. It is still worth taking a little extra time to ensure that you select the best for your model.

Card

The card used in many of these models is a dense hard surface type about 1mm in thickness. The corrugated type of card has limited use due to its inability to bend smoothly and a problem with waterproofing. Suitable card can often be obtained free from packaging or even the backs of old writing pads. Large sheets of card can be purchased from high street stationery shops or art shops. Sheets of good quality card might seem to be expensive but can be used to make several models, especially if you get into the habit of saving any offcuts.

The best way to use card is in large single pieces. If two pieces have to be joined, say to cover one side of a hull, then the joint should ideally occur over a bulkhead. This will reinforce the joint and prevent any cracks forming in use. If there is no convenient bulkhead to support the join, then use an internal card 'strap-glued' across the join.

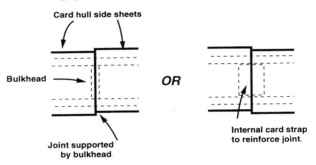

Cutting

It is possible to cut card with scissors but their shearing action can produce a deformed edge. A modelling knife with replaceable blades is the best way to cut both card and balsa. A razor blade can be far too dangerous and therefore ought to be avoided. One of the tricks to any successful cutting with one of these knives is to always change the blade as soon as it fails to cut cleanly. Far too many models, and modeller's fingers, have been damaged by trying to cut with a blunt blade.

A straight edge can only be cut using a rule. Metal rules are best as wood and plastic soon get damaged. Always cut with the rule between your fingers and the blade. Likewise, when cutting make sure that if the blade slips it cannot plunge into any part of your anatomy.

A cutting board is needed to support the item being cut and ought to be soft enough so as not to quickly blunt the blade. A flat sheet of softboard or the soft side of single surfaced hardboard can make a good cutting board. Commercial cutting boards with 'self-healing' plastic surfaces can make an excellent investment. Cutting out on the dining table is not recommended!

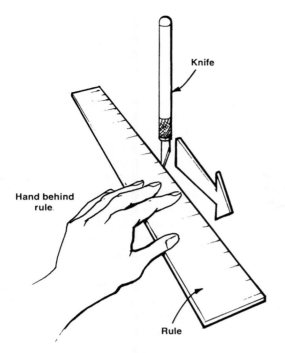

The actual technique of cutting can only be learnt through practice. The blade must be vertical to the surface you are cutting through. A good way to cut is to hold the knife like a pen, then 'draw' it along the rule. It is always better to make several light cuts along the same line than risk one heavy single cut.

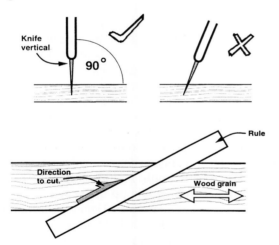

Card ought to cut evenly in all directions but balsawood has a distinct grain structure. This usually makes it easier to cut along the grain but harder to cut across. This can lead to the blade being deflected when cutting at an angle to the grain. If possible it is best to place the rule so that the blade cannot be so deflected.

Sanding

The edges and surfaces of balsa sheet and strip are usually supplied with a very smooth finish, however some sanding will still be needed especially on cut edges.

The correct method of sanding is to use a coarse paper to remove the bulk of the excess or defects, then smooth with a medium paper and finish off with a fine paper. Suitable packs of mixed sanding papers can be obtained in DIY shops. If you try to hold the paper in your hand while sanding then an irregular rather than flat surface will almost certainly be produced. A sanding block is the way to avoid this problem. I use a piece of wood about 25mm × 50mm × 150mm (1in. × 2in. × 6in.) in size around which the sandpaper is wrapped and held with drawing pins. This is convenient to hold, ensures a flat surface and saves your fingertips!

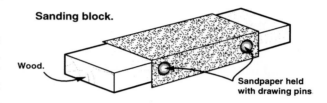

Adhesives and joints

The advent of rapid setting PVA woodglues has been a godsend for the modeller. The absence of smell, ease of wiping away mistakes and very strong final bond strength makes them ideal for card/balsa joints. Setting times of 15 to 30 minutes are quoted for the rapid types, which is more than adequate for long and/or tricky joints.

One drawback of PVA glues is that they are not waterproof although water-resistant types can be obtained. This is no great problem as the exterior surfaces ought to be well sealed and no significant amounts of water should enter the model while sailing.

The secret of good glued joints is that the two parts must fit closely together. Glue should never be used as a substitute for accurate cutting and building. Always check that the parts fit before applying glue – any excess can be sanded away while any gaps can be filled with slivers of wood.

Sufficient glue must be applied to one surface so that when pressed together, a continuous bead of glue can be seen on both sides of the joint. This

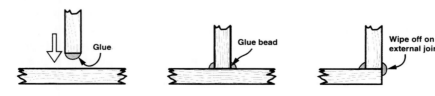

bead can be left on internal joints, often smoothed with a fingertip, but must be wiped off external surfaces.

Most glued joints in these models need to have the parts at right angles to each other. A small plastic set square can be ideal for checking this. When correctly aligned the parts can be held together using pins. Pins with large heads, e.g. map or dressmaking types, are ideal for this job.

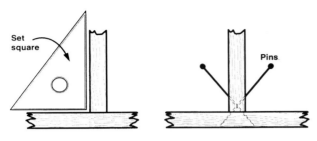

Only after the glue has fully hardened can the pins be removed. Sometimes the glue will firmly grip the pin and prevent its easy removal. Do not heave away on the pin as this can tear the balsa and/or card. Simply twist the head of the pin to break the bond between pin and glue, then pull the pin out.

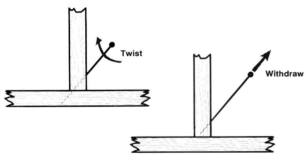

Finishing

Far too many modellers spoil their creations by rushing into the painting stage. No amount of paint can make up for poor construction and lack of surface preparation.

The first stage is to check for any small gaps or holes in the external surfaces of the model. Glue could be used to seal small defects but a filler may be needed on more substantial defects. A domestic filler, such as *Polyfilla*, is suitable as it bonds well to balsa–card structures and sands smooth to become invisible when painted. I find a tube of the ready-mixed filler to be most convenient.

Balsa and card will soak up water unless suitably sealed. A traditional, and still very effective, method is to use cellulose dope which is sold in most model shops and is widely used in building model aircraft. It readily penetrates into card and balsa to both toughen and seal the surface. Due to the solvent used it is very quick drying but very smelly and should never be used indoors. An alternative is domestic undercoat/primer – less smelly and cheaper than dope but its use indoors is still risky!

The same technique is used with either dope or primer. Both ought to be thinned for the first coats – a watery consistency is about right. This ensures that the first coats penetrate the porous surfaces to a greater depth and so produce a better sealing and strengthening effect. After each coat a slight surface roughness or 'fuzz' will be seen. This requires light sanding to remove. This effect will diminish with subsequent coats which can be of thicker consistency. Between 3 and 5 coats ought to produce a smooth surface with no evidence of the wood grain, joints, etc.

When painting you are advised to use a gloss type on the hull. This will give a tougher and more hardwearing surface than matt paints. The small tins of paint sold in model shops are of excellent quality and consistency provided you thoroughly stir the paint before use. Larger tins of domestic paints can be more economical but do remember to use liquid, not non-drip jelly types.

The paintbrush must be of good quality and large enough for the task. Painting with the wrong size brush, either too large for small areas or vice versa, is no fun at all. The brush must be clean and flexible, definitely not still stiff with paint from the previous job. Correct 'loading' of the brush occurs when no paint tries to drip off when moving between tin and model. A steady sweeping action should be used to cover the area evenly with the next line of paint just overlapping it. With many colours it is best to apply two or three thin coats, rather than a single thick one, which can produce a more solid colour and avoid any runs.

Straight lines between colours are best produced with masking tape. Plastic tape can also be used for trim details which would be hard to paint. Letters and numbers can be made up using self-adhesive packs sold in most stationers. Decorations can be protected by spraying the whole model with a can of clear varnish which can be gloss, satin or matt.

Propulsion

Small electric motors are used to power these models. A wide range of different makes are available but are often sold under their original three digit *Mabuchi* designations. They have a metal can type of body, usually with cooling vents at one end. The output shaft extends from one end and is about 10mm (⅜ in.) long. The individual plans specify the best type of motor to use. It is possible to use other motors but you need to avoid overpowering the smaller scale types of models.

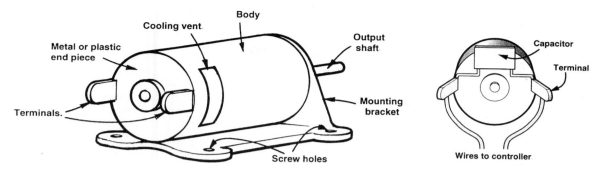

These motors are often sold with a mounting bracket fixed to the enclosed end of the motor case. The motor can be secured into a model by means of screws fitted through holes in the mounting bracket. The other end of the motor body is usually a plastic moulding which houses the rear bearing and the two terminals for connecting to the electrical circuit.

Modern R/C gear is very tolerant towards interference but any electrical motor used in a model ought to be suppressed. As the motor rotates small electrical arcs can form on the commutator and generate a radio signal. This is the same effect that some domestic appliances can produce on TV and radios. The usual symptom of such interference is that the servos work perfectly until the motor is switched on, then they jitter about. This problem can be avoided by soldering a small 0.01 to 0.05 microfarad capacitor between the motor terminals.

ter checking that the propeller can rotate freely. The motor is usually mounted with its shaft in line with the propeller shaft. An easy way to do this is to use scrap pieces of balsa packing under the motor mount then screw the motor into place. The coupling for small models can be made from some flexible tubing which is a tight push-fit onto both shafts. If a shaft is too small for the coupling tube then a piece of tight fitting tube can be pushed onto the shaft first, which will increase its diameter to grip the flexible tubing.

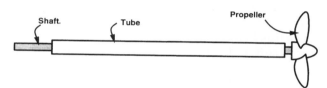

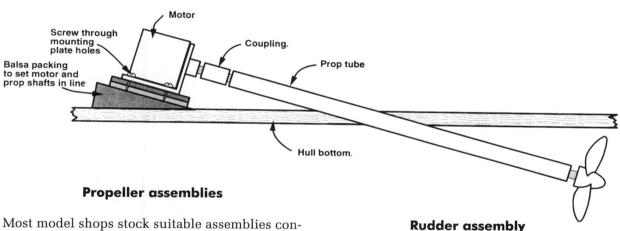

Propeller assemblies

Most model shops stock suitable assemblies consisting of a metal shaft with a propeller fitted to one end, the shaft running in a close-fitting tube. These are adequate for most small models but in fact you can easily make your own from wire and matching tube. More substantial propeller shafts and tubes are available for the more powerful models.

Installation

The propeller tube is fitted through a suitable hole made through the hull bottom and possibly a bulkhead. The tube should only be glued into place af-

Rudder assembly

Small commercial R/C rudder assemblies are available but it is not too difficult make up your own. The shaft needs to be a close fit into the hull-mounted tube, otherwise water can quickly creep inside the hull. The rudder blade can be cut from sheet metal – aluminium about 1.5mm (1/16 in.) thick is ideal – and secured with epoxy into a matching slot in the shaft. An alternative is to cut the blade shape from thinner aluminium sheet and epoxy it around the shaft. The lower end of the shaft must be bent into a 'U' shape to prevent the blade from rotating on the shaft.

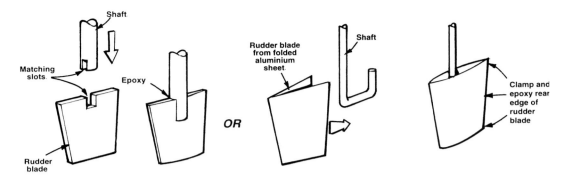

The tiller arm, for connecting the top of the rudder shaft with the servo, can also be a commercial item or home-made. A collet which matches the shaft simply needs an arm fixing to it. This must be strong enough for the loads applied when sailing otherwise control will be lost.

Radio installation

The rudder servo body must be secure and not able to move significantly or poor control will result. I usually screw the servo to a balsa rail or block which gives a firm but easy to remove installation. The link between servo and tiller arm can be made from stiff wire. This should not bend when operating and steel or brass wire about 1.5mm (¹⁄₁₆ in.) diameter is usually adequate. The one thing to ensure is that the servo and tiller arm are parallel when the rudder is in the neutral position. This produces an even movement when the rudder is operated.

The amount of rudder movement ought to be

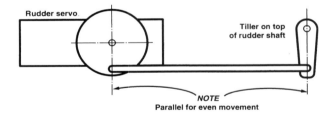

around 30 degrees either way to start with. This angle usually gives good steering without being too sensitive. More or less rudder movement can be obtained by moving the wire link to other holes in the servo and/or tiller arms. Do check that the rudder linkage cannot become jammed at the full rudder position.

The receiver aerial can be a problem with any model boat. It must never be left coiled up inside the hull or the effective radio range will be very short. For best results the aerial needs to be as vertical as possible. With most models it is usually enough to run the aerial through the deck or superstructure and then up over a mast. A small elastic band tied to the end of the aerial is often the most convenient way to apply a little tension. On many of my models I replace the end 20–30cm (8–12 inches) of the flexible aerial wire with a piece of fine stiff wire. This can be fitted vertically into the model's structure and results in out-of-sight radio range, even when I remember to wear my glasses! If you use a vertical wire then you must bend a safety loop on the end of the wire to avoid the risk of eye damage.

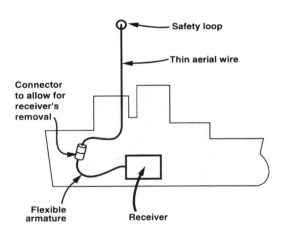

Batteries

The power for these models could be supplied from 'dry' battery packs and the best way is probably to use a commercial battery box which will hold the cells securely but allow for easy replacement. Provided the current drawn by the motor is not too large then dry cells can be a good idea. The best sizes to use would be the 'C' or 'D' cells – anything smaller will run down far too quickly and prove to be very expensive.

Rechargeable **nicad** cells are a sensible option as they can save money in the long run. They are virtually foolproof in operation provided you remember to fully recharge them before any sailing session.

With any type of battery you are strongly recommended to remove them from the model when not in use. This will avoid any corrosion problems that might occur inside a damp model. Also, when flat, dry cells can self-destruct in a very messy fashion.

Speed control

One of the great advantages of using electric power is the ease of controlling the model's speed. It is possible to make a simple switching system which gives FORWARD–STOP–REVERSE control of the motor. This does, however, waste the potential for fully variable speed control.

Most of the models in this book were fitted with a resistive control board which fits onto the top of a servo. Wiper arms, secured to the servo output disc or arm, move across the resistive tracks on the board and so allow the motor to speed up and slow down through several stages in both directions. They are very simple to install and maintain and the best known example of these boards in the UK is those sold under the name *Bob's Models* – check a current magazine for details of price.

Electronic speed controllers plug directly into the receiver and are then connected to both the battery and motor. They can offer infinitely variable motor speed although when installed in a model boat, the difference with resistance boards is not always apparent. The slightest mistake when connecting them to the battery pack can ruin an electronic controller, a mistake I have made a couple of times!

With motor controllers it is very much a case of 'paying your money and taking your choice'. One final piece of advice is to be careful if you are offered controllers intended for R/C aircraft or cars, they would probably lack the sensitivity required at the much lower power levels used by these small model boats.

Internal installation

How items are to be fitted inside a model depends upon the design of the model. A few important points do however apply to all models. Firstly, nothing should be able to move while sailing or the model's trim will alter. In the worst case a model could flounder. Also, wires or linkages must not jam or foul the operation of anything inside the model. Losing power or control of a model can lead to the loss of the whole model. Finally, any ballast must be fitted as low inside the model as possible to ensure positive stability.

Building time!

The nine model plans that follow are not supplied with individual detailed building notes. Each plan was drawn to include specific information on construction and outfitting. If you are unsure about any stage then refer to the previous notes.

All relevant structural parts are drawn full size. Slight variations in shape and size are unlikely to be critical *but* the hull must be square and true. All the glued joints must be a good fit to achieve maximum strength.

With most models it is best to install the propeller tube, shaft, motor and coupling *before* adding the hull sides. Likewise, the rudder tube, servo and linkage ought to installed at this stage. This will greatly ease the task of getting everything correctly lined up. It may be better to remove the motor, propeller shaft, rudder and servo before completing the hull construction – getting glue all over these items is not good news.

The materials needed to build the basic structure of the model are given for each plan. You may well be able to economise by using material left over from other models. A little ingenuity will be able to supply many of the smaller details.

As stated previously, there is no reason why these plans cannot be altered to suit personal tastes. Also, if you have other items available then alternative motors and batteries could be used.

THE MODELS

ARCADY

Tugs have excellent proportions for working models offering a capacious hull even when reduced to small sizes. This model is a little different from the usual tugs in being based on those used by the American Leigh Valley Railroad.

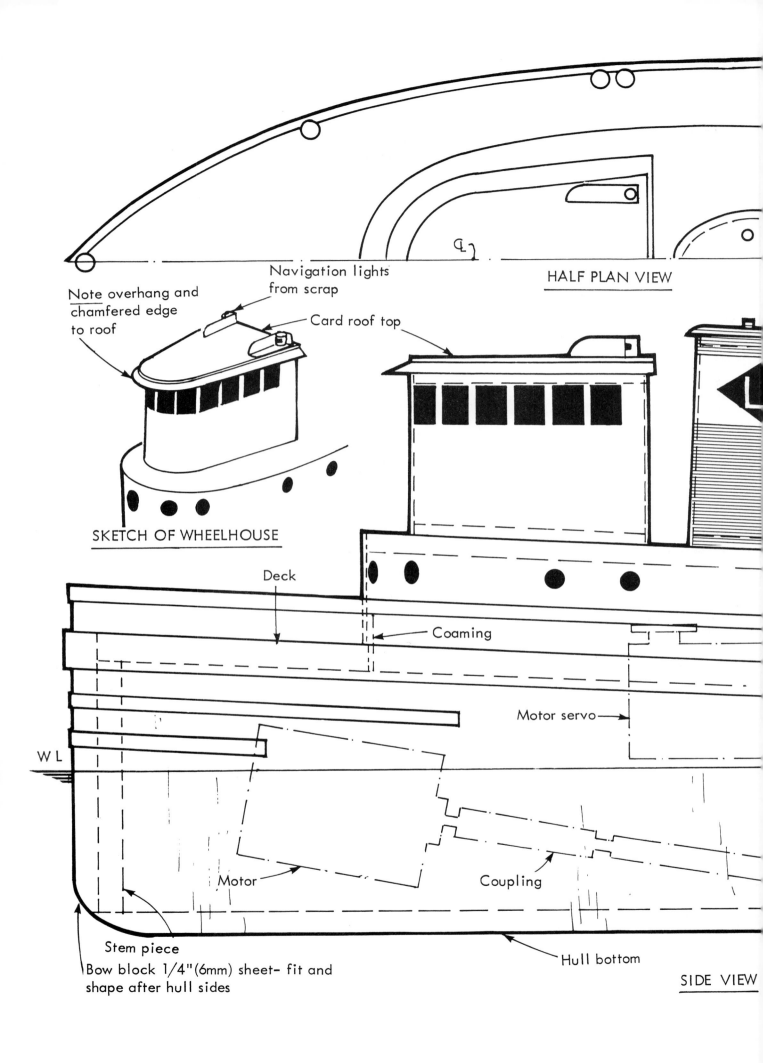

HALF PLAN VIEW

Navigation lights
from scrap

Note overhang and
chamfered edge
to roof

Card roof top

SKETCH OF WHEELHOUSE

Deck

Coaming

Motor servo

W L

Motor

Coupling

Stem piece

Bow block 1/4"(6mm) sheet- fit and
shape after hull sides

Hull bottom

SIDE VIEW

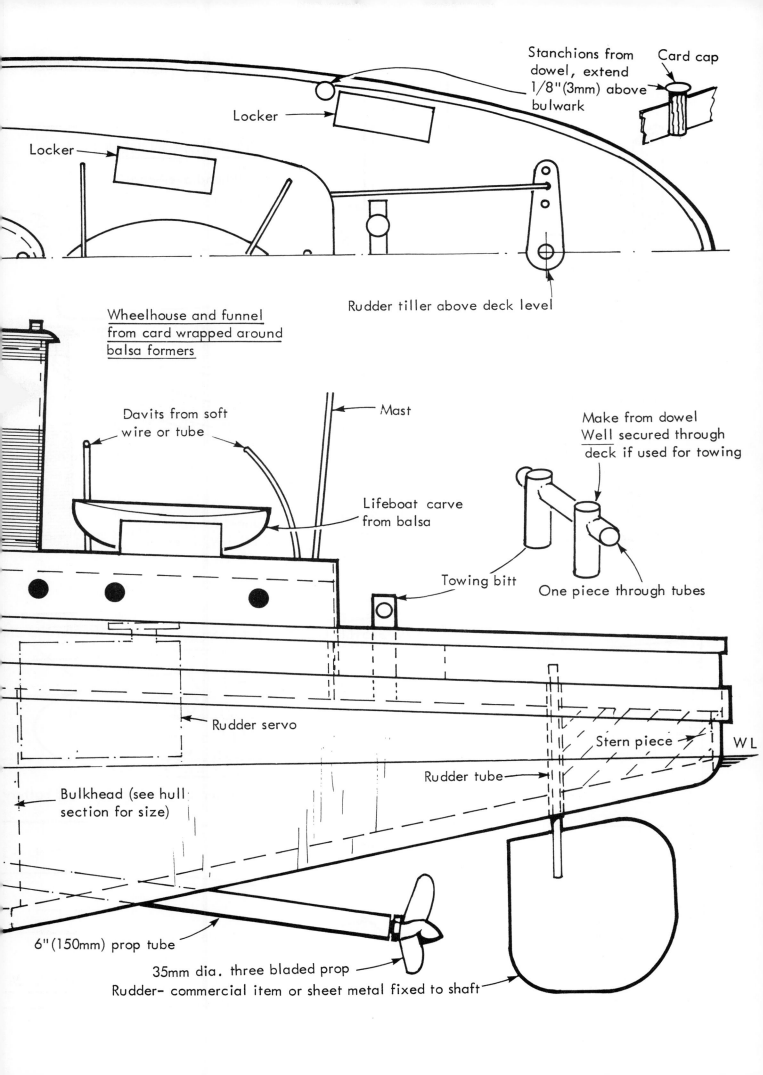

Stanchions from dowel, extend 1/8"(3mm) above bulwark

Card cap

Locker

Locker

Rudder tiller above deck level

Wheelhouse and funnel from card wrapped around balsa formers

Davits from soft wire or tube

Mast

Make from dowel Well secured through deck if used for towing

Lifeboat carve from balsa

Towing bitt

One piece through tubes

Rudder servo

Stern piece

WL

Rudder tube

Bulkhead (see hull section for size)

6"(150mm) prop tube

35mm dia. three bladed prop

Rudder- commercial item or sheet metal fixed to shaft

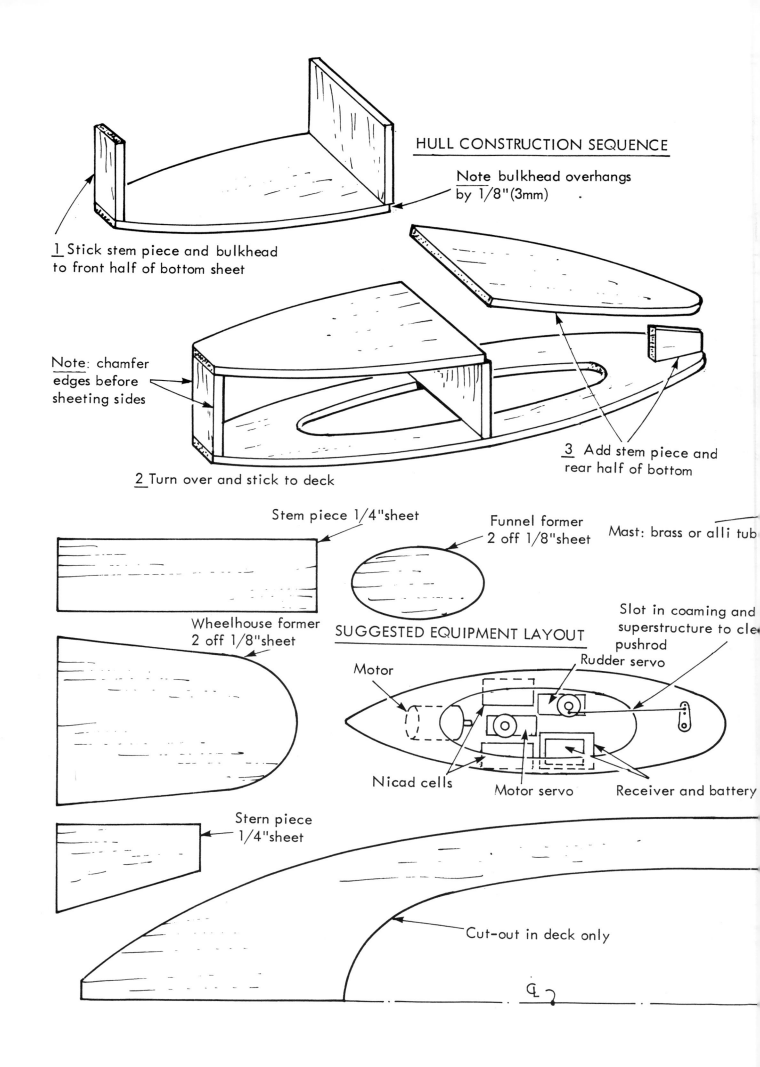

HULL CONSTRUCTION SEQUENCE

Note bulkhead overhangs by 1/8"(3mm).

1 Stick stem piece and bulkhead to front half of bottom sheet

Note: chamfer edges before sheeting sides

2 Turn over and stick to deck

3 Add stem piece and rear half of bottom

Stem piece 1/4"sheet

Funnel former 2 off 1/8"sheet

Mast: brass or alli tub

Wheelhouse former 2 off 1/8"sheet

SUGGESTED EQUIPMENT LAYOUT

Slot in coaming and superstructure to clear pushrod

Motor

Rudder servo

Nicad cells

Motor servo

Receiver and battery

Stern piece 1/4"sheet

Cut-out in deck only

9

Deck

Hull bottom

1/4"(6mm) sheet

Save cut-out for superstructure

To make identical bottom and deck pieces, use template on one side then turn over for other

Wire solder or epoxy to rear of mast

HULL SECTION SHOWING BASIC CONSTRUCTION

Towing lights

Railings around superstructure staunchions from wire epoxied into hull, rails from wire soldered to staunchions (not shown on side view)

1/4"(6mm) sheet from deck cut-out

Removable superstructure, sides from card- close fit over deck coaming

Wire soldered or epoxied to tube

Deck

Hull sides above waterline plated with card

Card deck coaming

Protective fenders from card

Bulkhead from 1/4"(6mm) sheet

Hull sides 1/8"(3mm) sheet grain vertical

Hole for prop tube

Template for hull bottom and deck

Corner rounded

Hull bottom

Before shqping

Cut line for bottom only

Basic materials

- One sheet ¼ × 4 inch (6 × 100 millimetre) balsa
- One sheet ⅛ × 3 inch (3 × 75 millimetre) balsa
- 6 inch (150 millimetre) long propeller shaft and tube
- One Mabuchi-style 360, 380 or 385 motor

Colour scheme

Hull	below waterline	black
	above waterline	green
Decks	grey	
Superstructure	red	
Funnel	black with red band containing black diamond with yellow letters	

Battery

With the suggested motors 2–3 nicad cells of capacity 1.2–2 Ah are adequate. Too much power results in a hard to handle model.

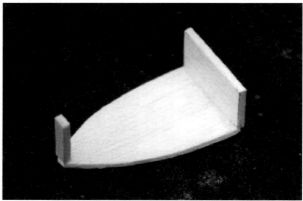

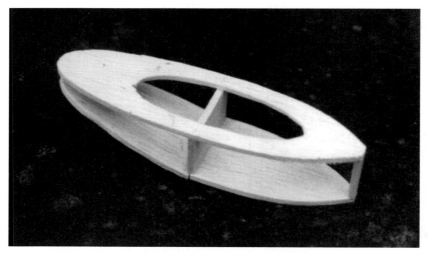

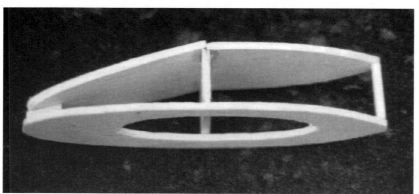

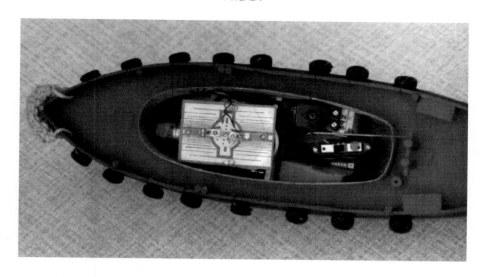

TALISMAN

Fishing boats make attractive models at any size. *Talisman's* modest dimensions still give a displacement of 2–2½ pounds (1kg) which is more than enough for standard R/C gear and an adequate battery.

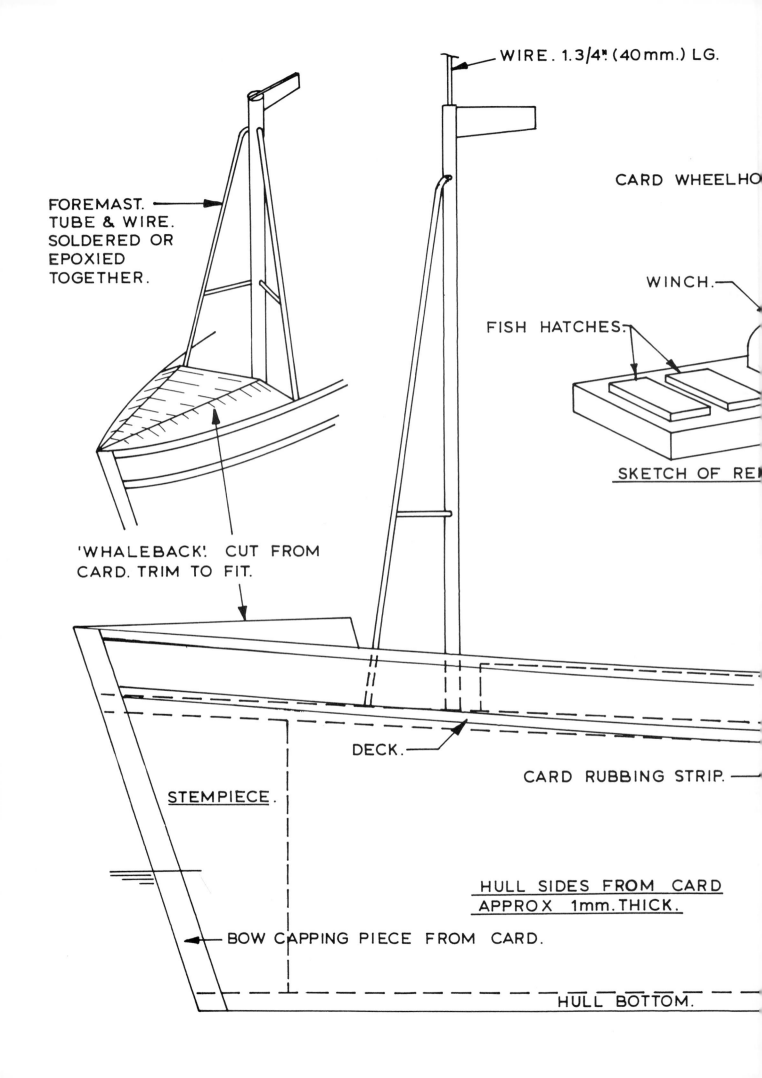

FOREMAST.
TUBE & WIRE.
SOLDERED OR
EPOXIED
TOGETHER.

WIRE. 1.3/4" (40 mm.) LG.

CARD WHEELHO

WINCH.

FISH HATCHES.

SKETCH OF RE

'WHALEBACK'. CUT FROM
CARD. TRIM TO FIT.

DECK.

CARD RUBBING STRIP.

STEMPIECE.

HULL SIDES FROM CARD
APPROX 1mm.THICK.

BOW CAPPING PIECE FROM CARD.

HULL BOTTOM.

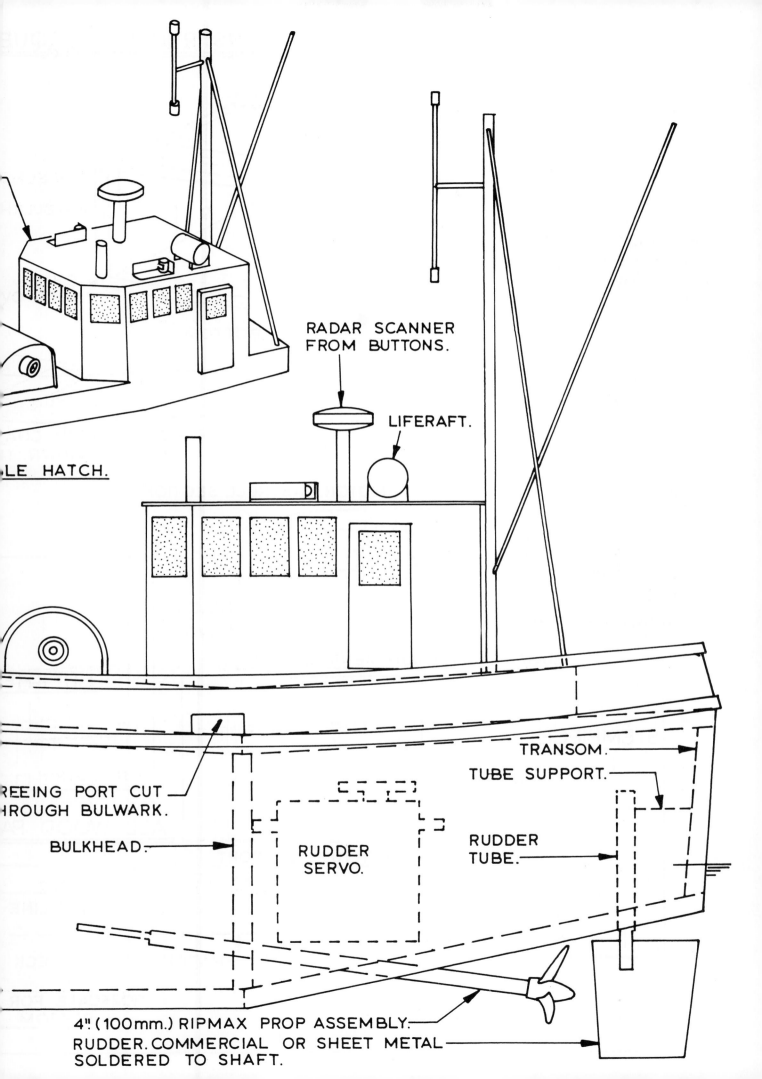

RADAR SCANNER
FROM BUTTONS.

LIFERAFT.

LE HATCH.

TRANSOM.

TUBE SUPPORT.

REEING PORT CUT
HROUGH BULWARK.

BULKHEAD.

RUDDER
SERVO.

RUDDER
TUBE.

4" (100 mm.) RIPMAX PROP ASSEMBLY.
RUDDER. COMMERCIAL OR SHEET METAL
SOLDERED TO SHAFT.

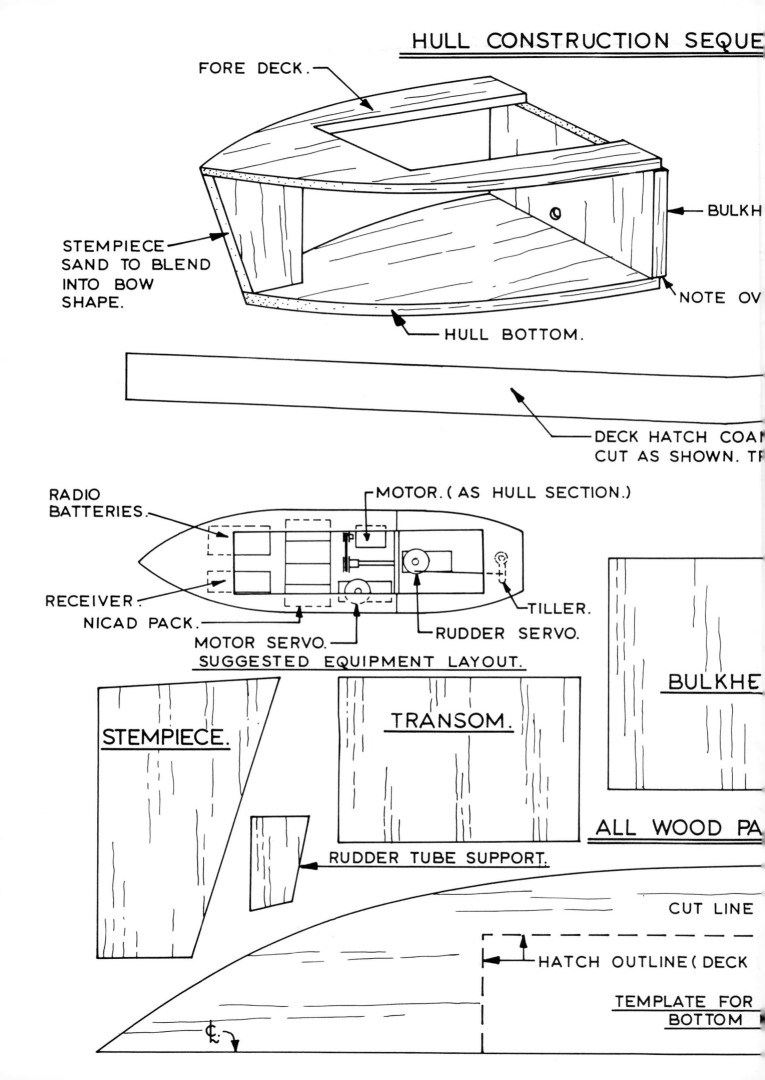

FORE DECK.

BULKH

STEMPIECE
SAND TO BLEND
INTO BOW
SHAPE.

NOTE OV

HULL BOTTOM.

DECK HATCH COAM
CUT AS SHOWN. T

RADIO
BATTERIES.

MOTOR. (AS HULL SECTION.)

RECEIVER.

TILLER.

NICAD PACK.

RUDDER SERVO.

MOTOR SERVO.

SUGGESTED EQUIPMENT LAYOUT.

BULKHE

STEMPIECE.

TRANSOM.

ALL WOOD PA

RUDDER TUBE SUPPORT.

CUT LINE

HATCH OUTLINE(DECK

TEMPLATE FOR
BOTTOM

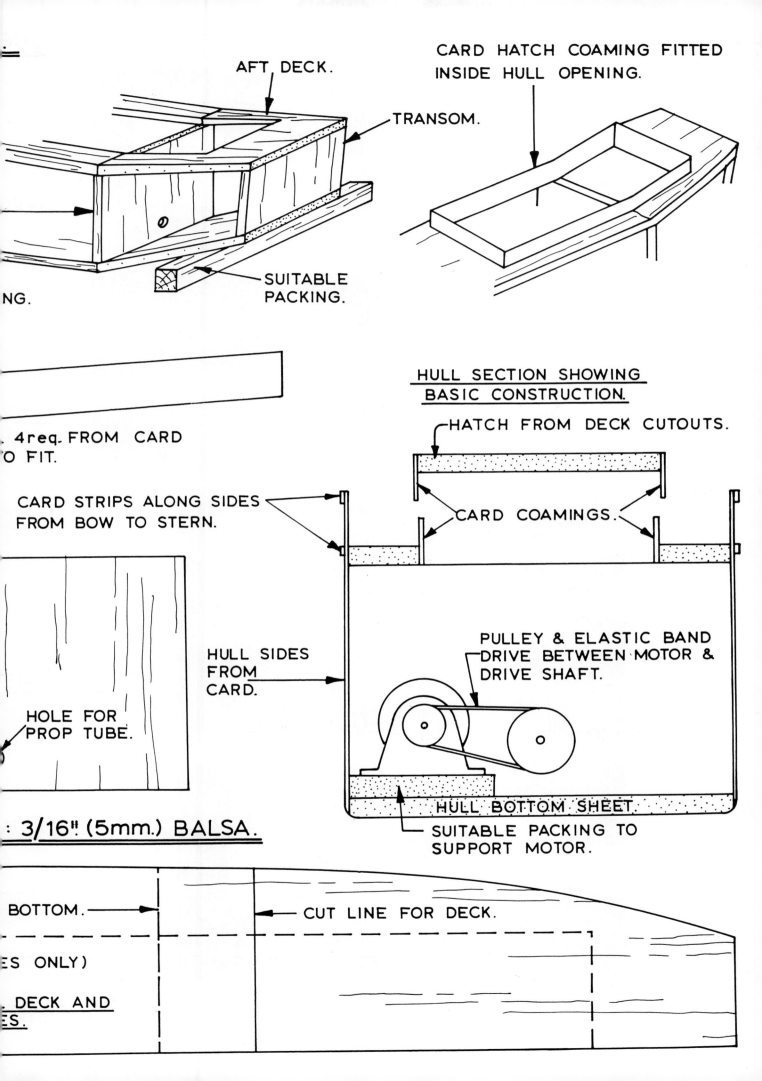

AFT DECK.

TRANSOM.

CARD HATCH COAMING FITTED
INSIDE HULL OPENING.

SUITABLE
PACKING.

NG.

4 req. FROM CARD
O FIT.

CARD STRIPS ALONG SIDES
FROM BOW TO STERN.

HOLE FOR
PROP TUBE.

: 3/16" (5mm.) BALSA.

HULL SECTION SHOWING
BASIC CONSTRUCTION.

HATCH FROM DECK CUTOUTS.

CARD COAMINGS.

HULL SIDES
FROM
CARD.

PULLEY & ELASTIC BAND
DRIVE BETWEEN MOTOR &
DRIVE SHAFT.

HULL BOTTOM SHEET.

SUITABLE PACKING TO
SUPPORT MOTOR.

BOTTOM.

CUT LINE FOR DECK.

S ONLY)

DECK AND
S.

Basic materials

- One sheet ³⁄₁₆ × 4 inch (5 – 100 millimetre) balsa
- Card sheet 1mm thick
- 4 inch (100 millimetre) long propeller shaft and tube
- One Mabuchi-style 260 or 360 motor

Colour scheme

Hull	below waterline	brick red
	above waterline	black
Deck	green	
Hatch	grey and brown	
Wheelhouse	sides	grey
	roof	white
Rubbing strips	white	

Battery

3–4 nicad cells of capacity 1.2 Ah ought to give good speed and endurance.

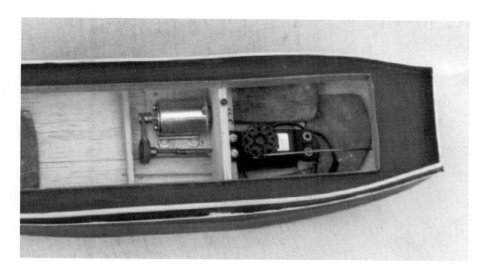

KNOCKER WHITE

This model is based on the traditional style of tug used by Whites Towage of London. The deck is made in three sections to produce the desired hull sheerline.

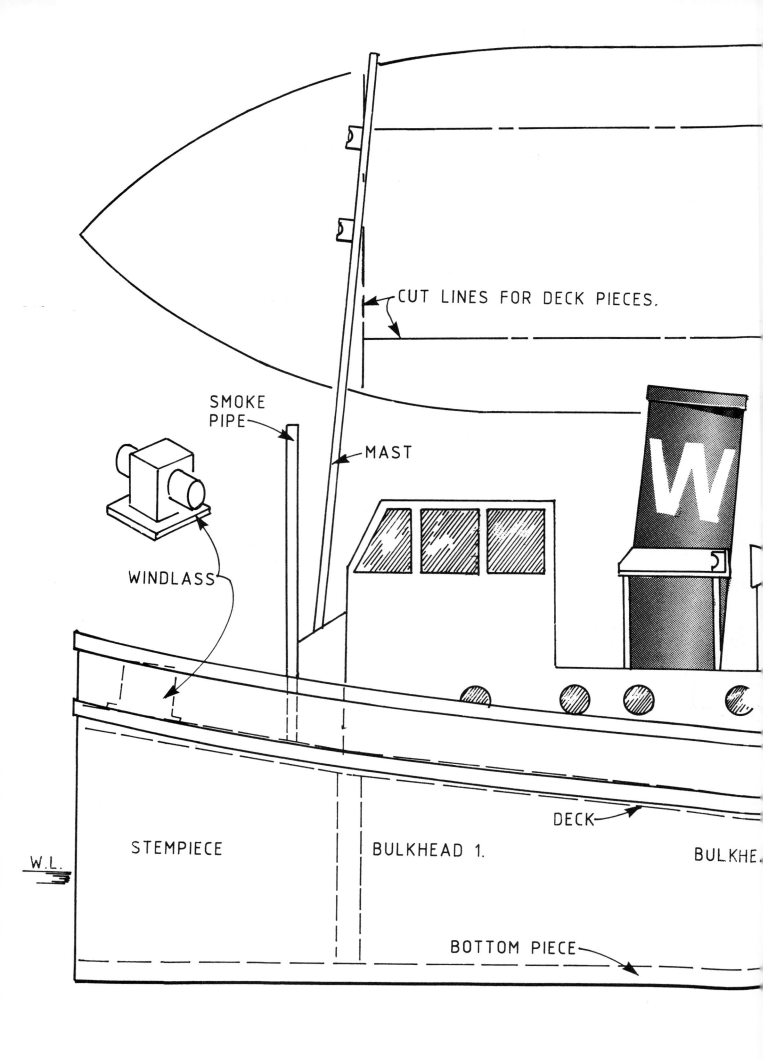

CUT LINES FOR DECK PIECES.

SMOKE
PIPE

MAST

WINDLASS

W

DECK

W.L.

STEMPIECE

BULKHEAD 1.

BULKHE

BOTTOM PIECE

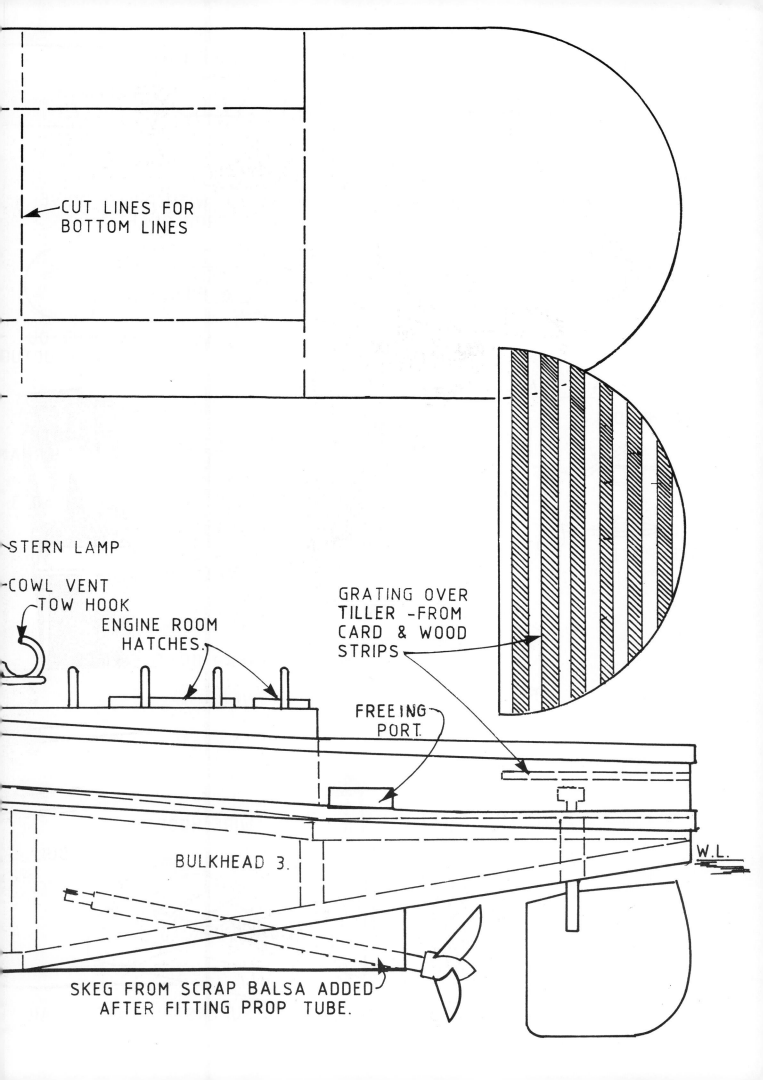

CUT LINES FOR
BOTTOM LINES

STERN LAMP

COWL VENT

TOW HOOK

ENGINE ROOM
HATCHES.

GRATING OVER
TILLER -FROM
CARD & WOOD
STRIPS

FREEING
PORT.

BULKHEAD 3.

W.L.

SKEG FROM SCRAP BALSA ADDED
AFTER FITTING PROP TUBE.

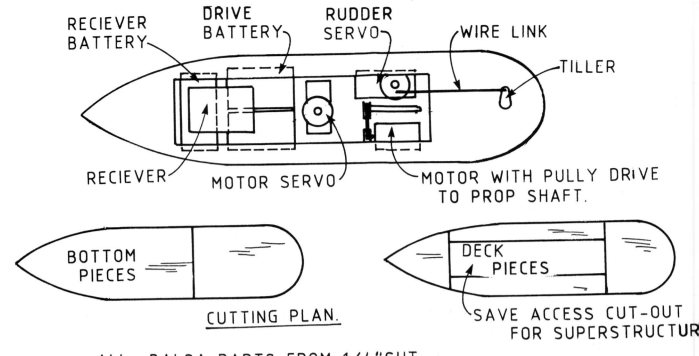

RECIEVER BATTERY
DRIVE BATTERY
RUDDER SERVO
WIRE LINK
TILLER
RECIEVER
MOTOR SERVO
MOTOR WITH PULLY DRIVE TO PROP SHAFT.

BOTTOM PIECES

CUTTING PLAN.

DECK PIECES

SAVE ACCESS CUT-OUT FOR SUPERSTRUCTUR

ALL BALSA PARTS FROM 1/4"SHT.

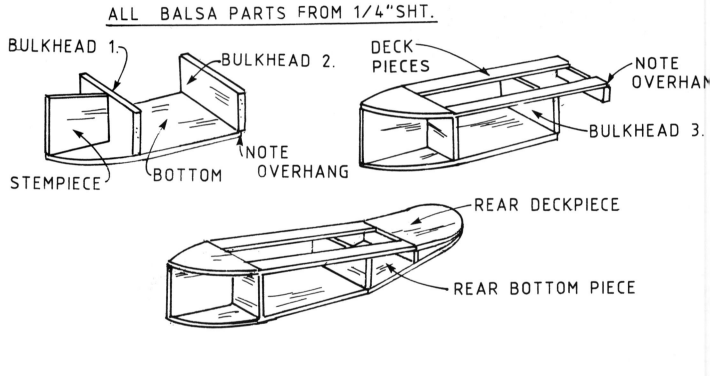

BULKHEAD 1.
BULKHEAD 2.
DECK PIECES
NOTE OVERHAN
BULKHEAD 3.
STEMPIECE
BOTTOM
NOTE OVERHANG

REAR DECKPIECE
REAR BOTTOM PIECE

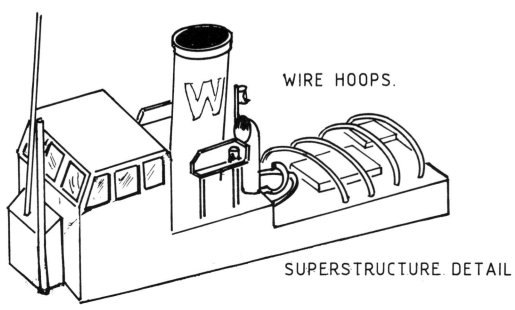

WIRE HOOPS.

SUPERSTRUCTURE DETAIL

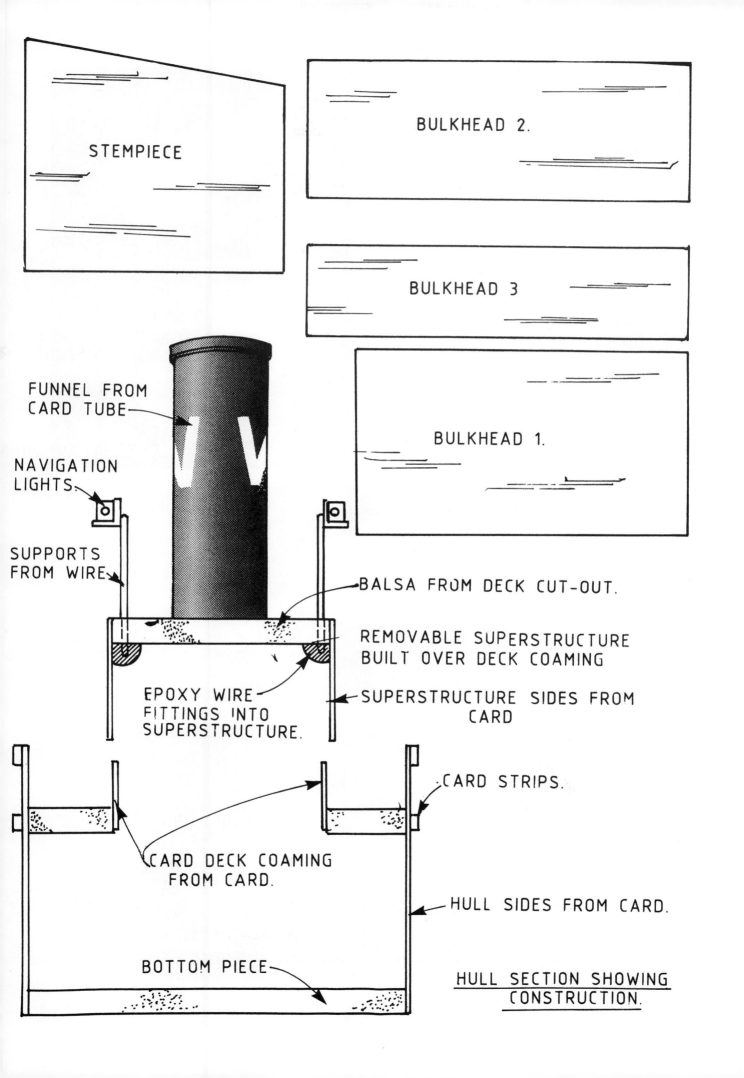

STEMPIECE

BULKHEAD 2.

BULKHEAD 3

BULKHEAD 1.

FUNNEL FROM
CARD TUBE

NAVIGATION
LIGHTS.

SUPPORTS
FROM WIRE

BALSA FROM DECK CUT-OUT.

REMOVABLE SUPERSTRUCTURE
BUILT OVER DECK COAMING

EPOXY WIRE
FITTINGS INTO
SUPERSTRUCTURE.

SUPERSTRUCTURE SIDES FROM
CARD

CARD STRIPS.

CARD DECK COAMING
FROM CARD.

HULL SIDES FROM CARD.

BOTTOM PIECE

HULL SECTION SHOWING
CONSTRUCTION.

Basic materials

- One sheet ¼ × 4 inch (6 × 100 millimetre) balsa
- Card sheet 1mm thick
- 4 inch (100 millimetre) long propeller shaft and tube
- One Mabuchi-style 260 or 360 motor

Colour scheme

Hull	below waterline brick red
	above waterline black
Deck	brick red
Inside bulwarks	brown
Superstructure	brown
Funnel	black with white 'W'

Battery

3–4 nicad cells of capacity 1.2 Ah ought to match this model.

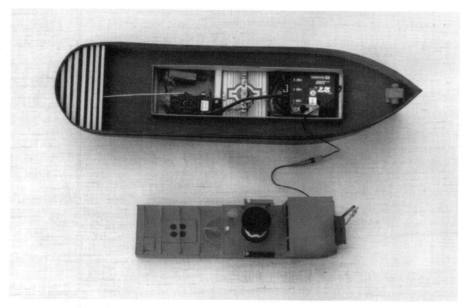

YSD

This model is a little different being based upon a self-propelled derrick used by the US Navy in the Second World War. These boats were often employed to transfer damaged and replacement aircraft between ships and shore. This gives you the excuse to build a suitable 1/72 scale aircraft kit.

The limited access into the hull means that the motor and coupling must be 100% reliable. All wiring to the motor must be in place before adding the side sheeting. If required, extra internal volume can easily be obtained by increasing the depth of the bulkheads and stempiece.

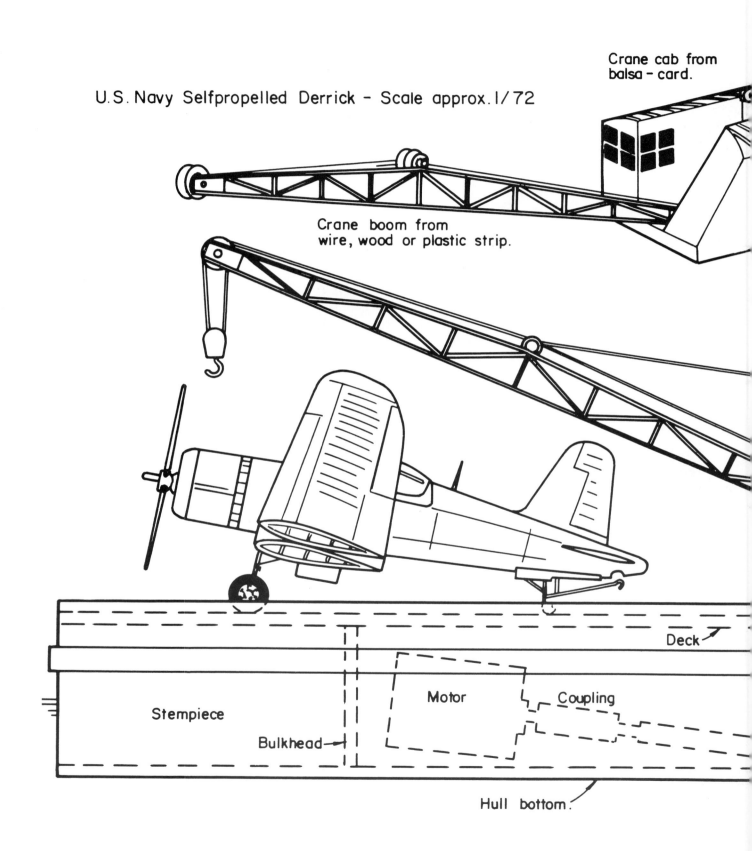

U.S. Navy Selfpropelled Derrick — Scale approx. 1/72

Crane cab from
balsa - card.

Crane boom from
wire, wood or plastic strip.

Deck

Stempiece

Bulkhead

Motor

Coupling

Hull bottom.

Suggested Internal Layout

Motor
Receiver batteries
Receiver
Tiller arm wire link to servo.
Motor batteries.
Motor servo
Rudder servo.

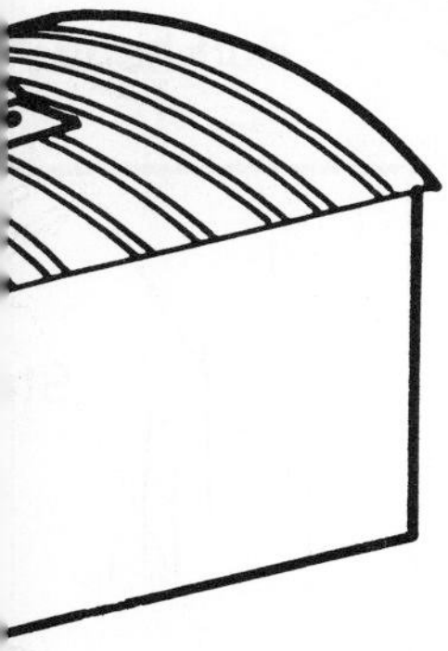

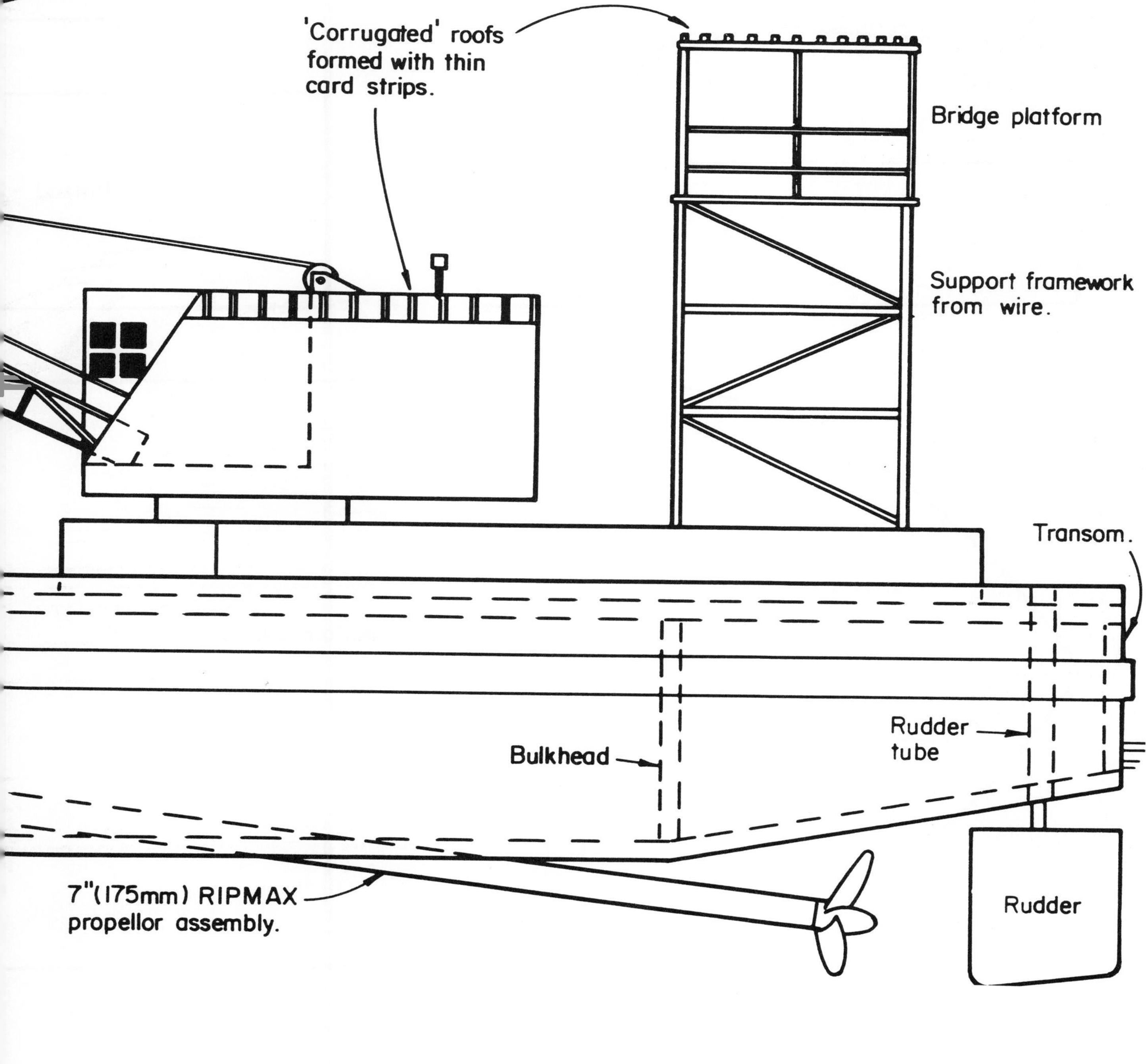

'Corrugated' roofs formed with thin card strips.
Bridge platform
Support framework from wire.
Transom.
Rudder tube
Bulkhead
7"(175mm) RIPMAX propellor assembly.
Rudder

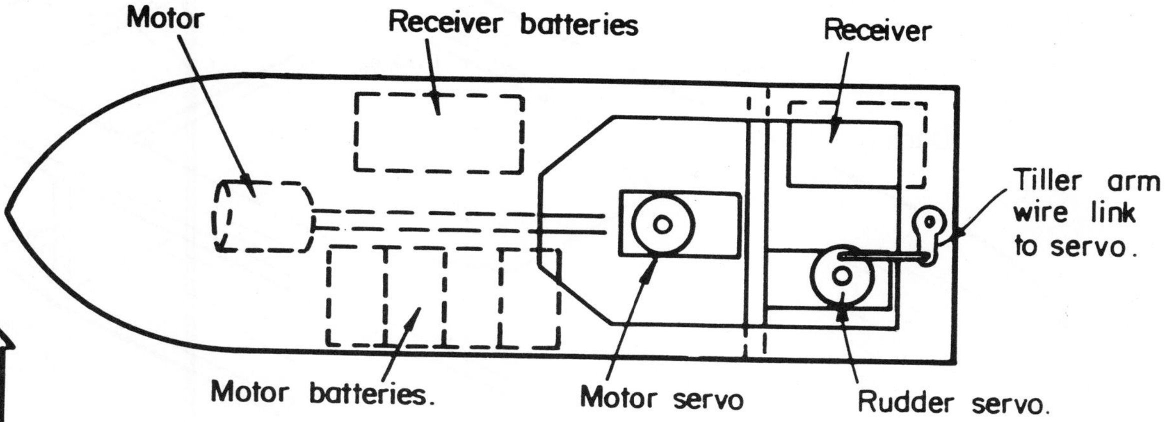

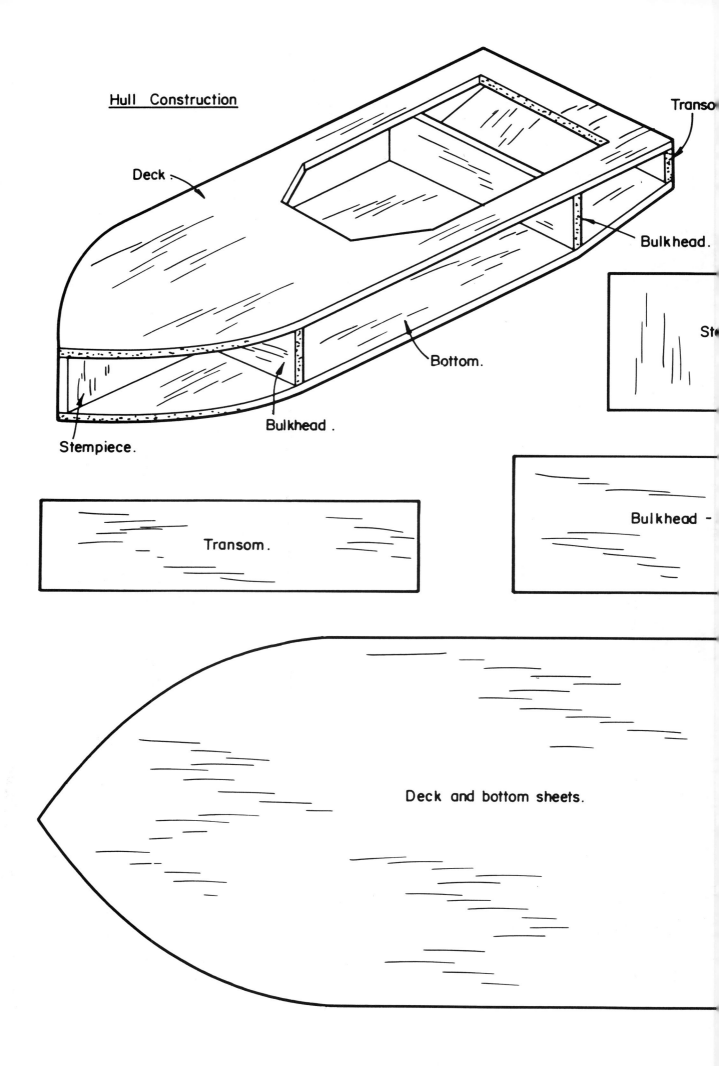

Hull Construction

Deck.

Transo[m]

Bulkhead.

Bottom.

Bulkhead.

Stempiece.

St[em]

Transom.

Bulkhead -

Deck and bottom sheets.

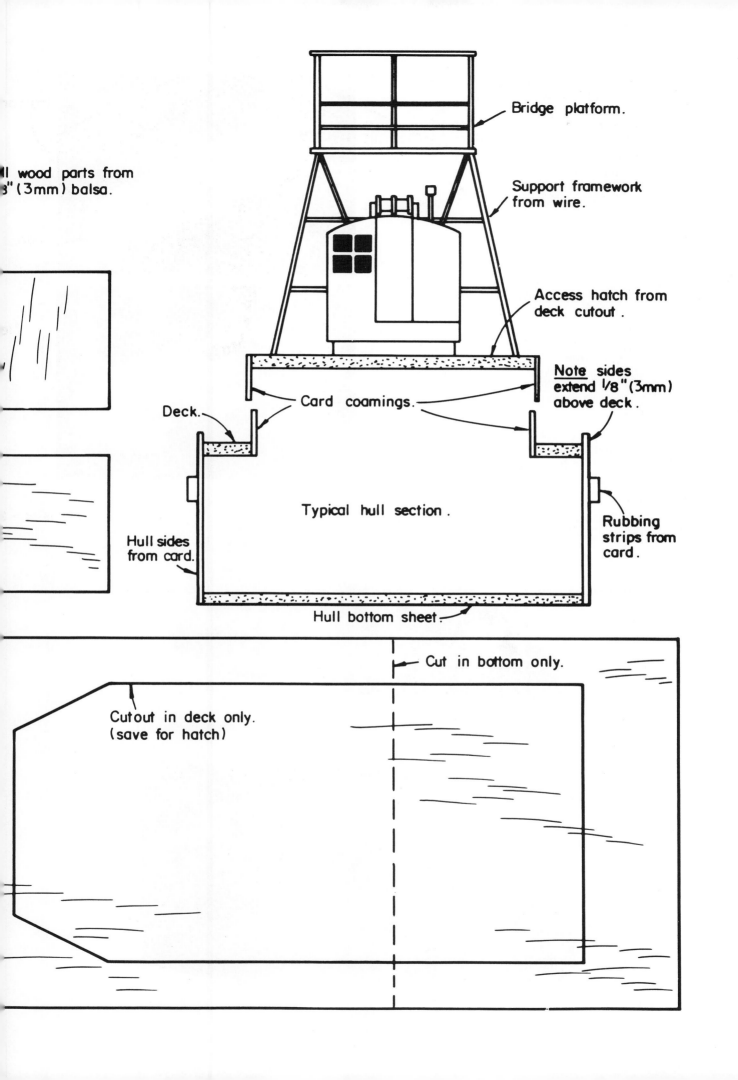

ll wood parts from
3" (3mm) balsa.

Bridge platform.

Support framework
from wire.

Access hatch from
deck cutout.

Note sides
extend 1/8" (3mm)
above deck.

Deck.

Card coamings.

Typical hull section.

Rubbing
strips from
card.

Hull sides
from card.

Hull bottom sheet.

Cut in bottom only.

Cutout in deck only.
(save for hatch)

Basic materials

- One sheet ⅛ × 4 inch (3 × 100 millimetre) balsa
- Card sheet 1mm thick
- 7 inch (180 millimetre) long propeller shaft and tube
- One Mabuchi-style 360 or 385 motor

Colour scheme

Hull	below waterline	brick red
	above waterline	medium grey
Deck	dark grey	
Superstructure and crane	medium grey	

Battery

Only modest power is required for this model, so 2–4 nicad cells dependent upon the motor used will be adequate.

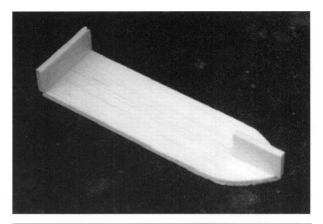

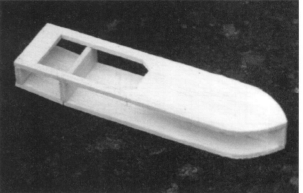

BREDETTE

After tugs, lifeboats must be the next most popular subjects for working models. This model is loosely based upon the fast Brede class used by the RNLI. The hard chine style of hull allows the model to operate safely at higher speeds than previous designs in this book.

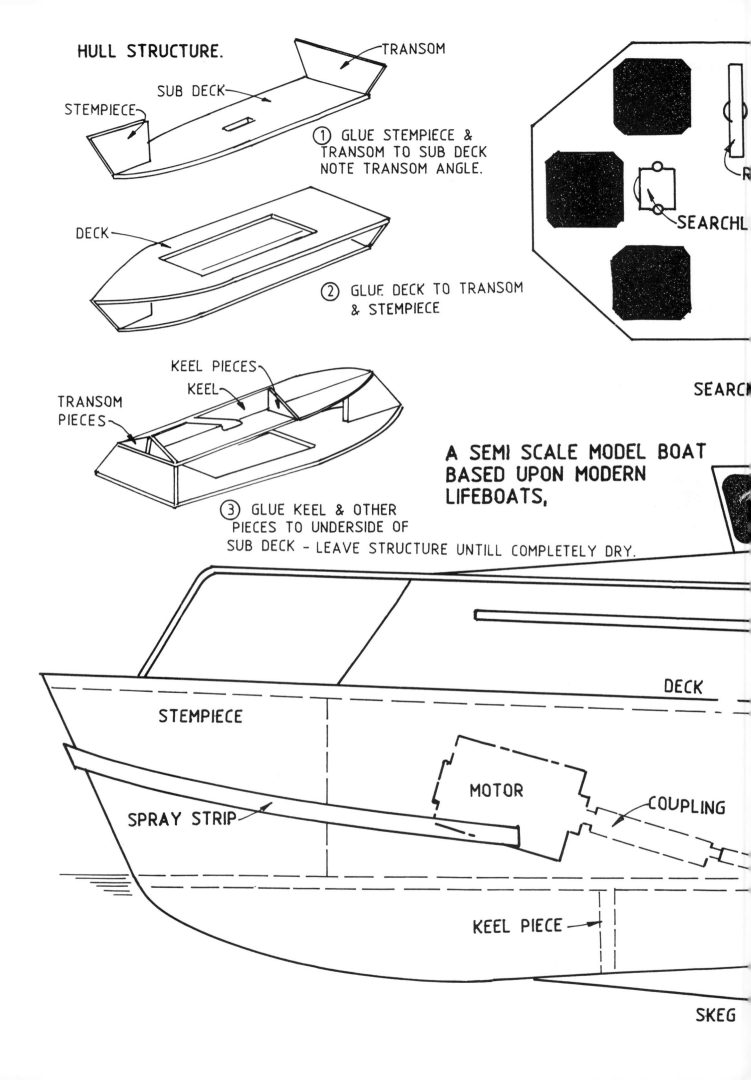

HULL STRUCTURE.

TRANSOM

SUB DECK

STEMPIECE

① GLUE STEMPIECE &
TRANSOM TO SUB DECK
NOTE TRANSOM ANGLE.

DECK

② GLUE DECK TO TRANSOM
& STEMPIECE

SEARCHL

KEEL PIECES
KEEL

TRANSOM
PIECES

③ GLUE KEEL & OTHER
PIECES TO UNDERSIDE OF
SUB DECK - LEAVE STRUCTURE UNTILL COMPLETELY DRY.

SEARC

A SEMI SCALE MODEL BOAT
BASED UPON MODERN
LIFEBOATS,

DECK

STEMPIECE

MOTOR

COUPLING

SPRAY STRIP

KEEL PIECE

SKEG

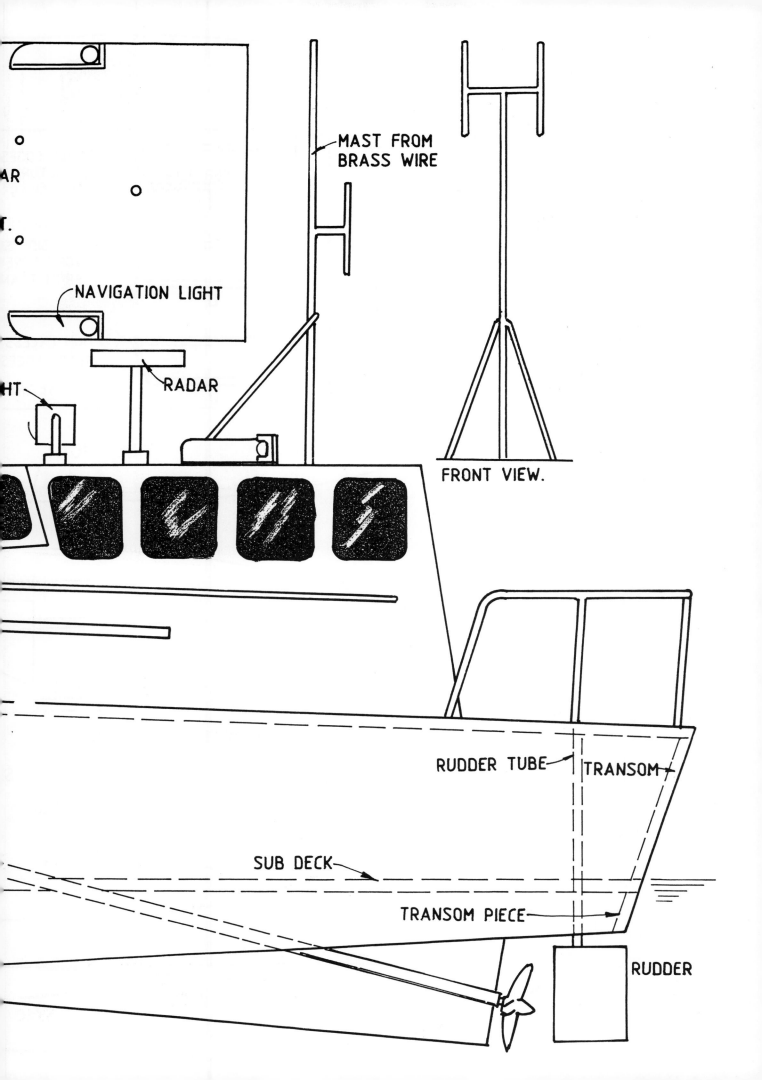

MAST FROM
BRASS WIRE

NAVIGATION LIGHT

RADAR

FRONT VIEW.

RUDDER TUBE   TRANSOM

SUB DECK

TRANSOM PIECE

RUDDER

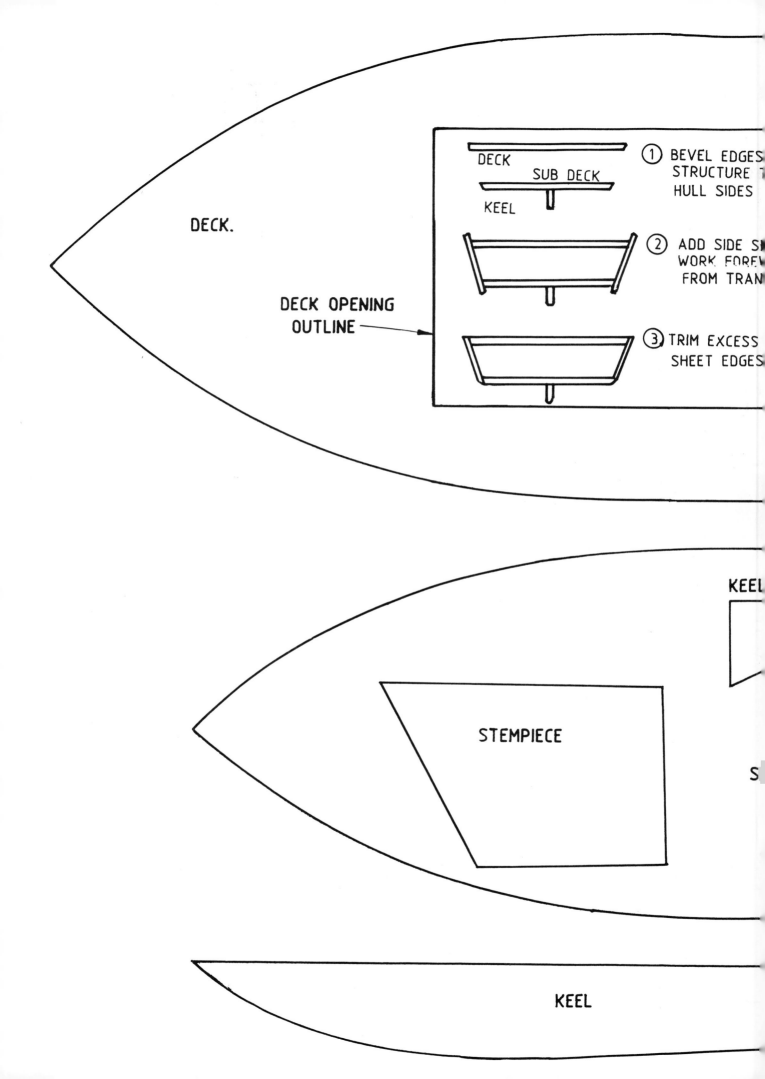

DECK.

DECK OPENING
OUTLINE

DECK
SUB DECK
KEEL

① BEVEL EDGES
STRUCTURE
HULL SIDES

② ADD SIDE S
WORK FOREW
FROM TRAN

③ TRIM EXCESS
SHEET EDGES

KEEL

STEMPIECE

S

KEEL

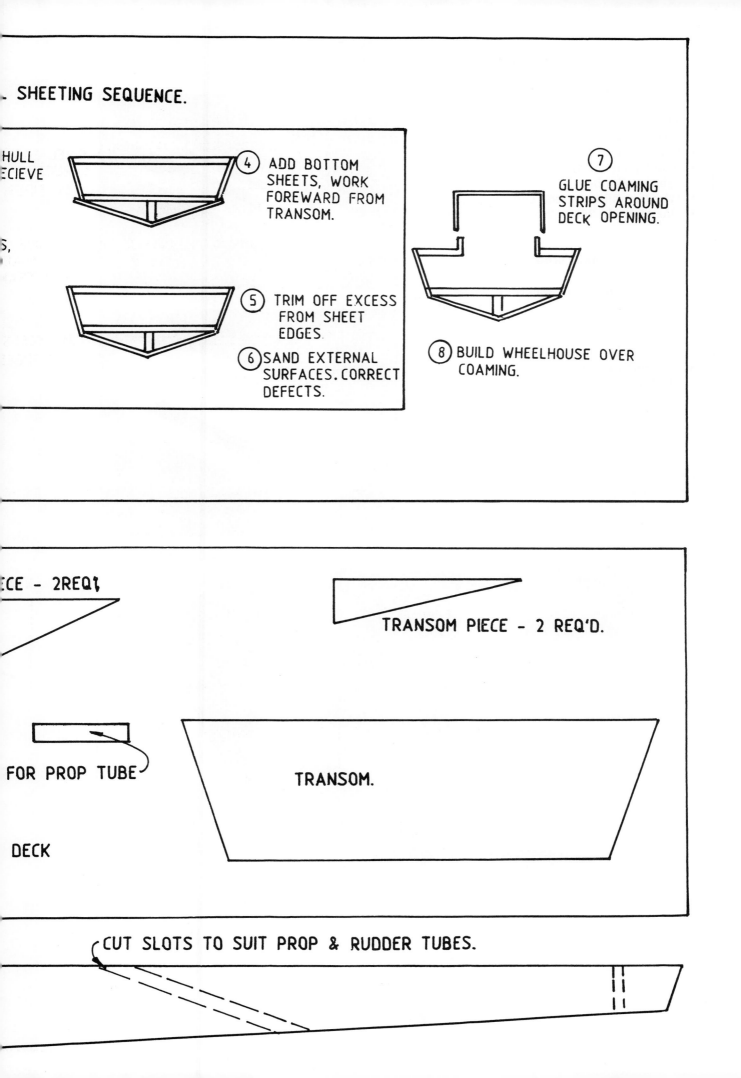

SHEETING SEQUENCE.

HULL
ECIEVE

4 ADD BOTTOM
SHEETS, WORK
FOREWARD FROM
TRANSOM.

5 TRIM OFF EXCESS
FROM SHEET
EDGES.

6 SAND EXTERNAL
SURFACES. CORRECT
DEFECTS.

7 GLUE COAMING
STRIPS AROUND
DECK OPENING.

8 BUILD WHEELHOUSE OVER
COAMING.

CE - 2REQ!

TRANSOM PIECE - 2 REQ'D.

FOR PROP TUBE

TRANSOM.

DECK

CUT SLOTS TO SUIT PROP & RUDDER TUBES.

Basic materials

- Three sheets ⅛ × 4 inch (3 × 100 millimetre) balsa
- Card sheet 1mm thick
- 6 inch (150 millimetre) long propeller
  shaft and tube
- Wire (for railings) – soft copper or brass
- One Mabuchi 380 or 'Speed 400' motor

Colour scheme

Hull	below waterline	gloss dull red
	above waterline	gloss blue
Deck	matt dark grey	
Superstructure	orange	
Hull bands	red and white self-adhesive tape	

Battery

With the suggested motors, 4 nicad cells of capacity 1.2 to 2 Ah capacity ought to have the
model running at a fast but safe speed.

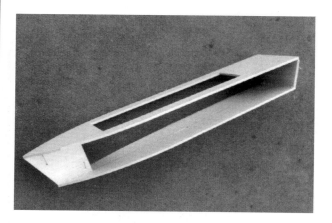

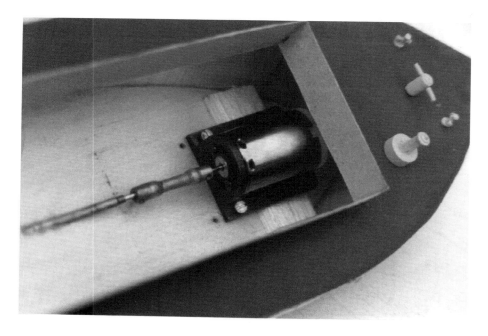

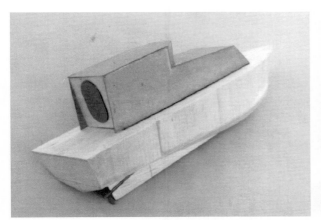

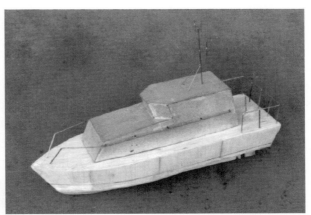

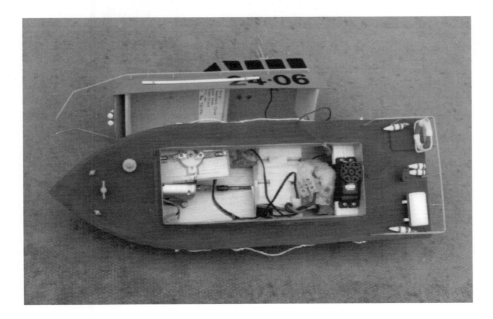

JENNY SUE

This is a tug with a difference! It is based upon the North American style of river push tugs. The angular lines of these vessels allow you to build the model to a large scale enabling you to add details without it becoming fragile – you can even add a crew of plastic figures!

The model is intended to be sailed with twin independently controlled motors for both propulsion and steerage. This requires you to use the transmitter sticks in 'tank' fashion. A transmitter with twin dual axis stick units is ideal but many two function outfits can, with care, have the rudder stick turned through 90 degrees. Alternatively, a conventional rudder system could be fitted with either single or twin access.

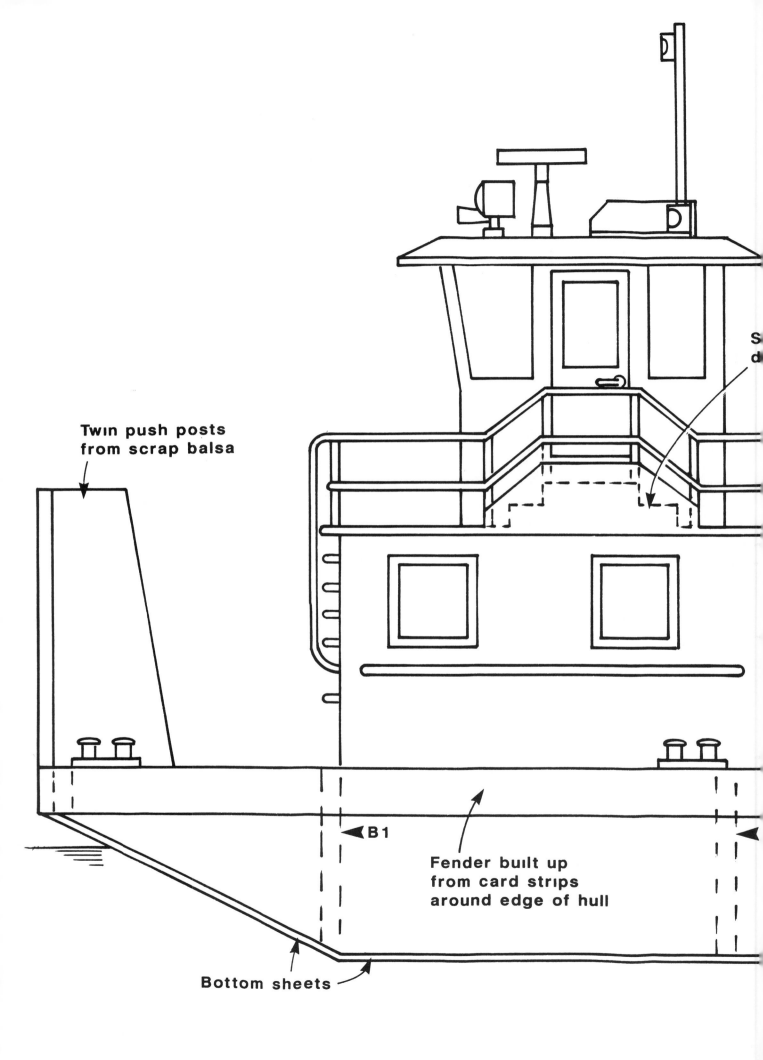

**Twin push posts
from scrap balsa**

S
d

◄ B1

**Fender built up
from card strips
around edge of hull**

◄

Bottom sheets

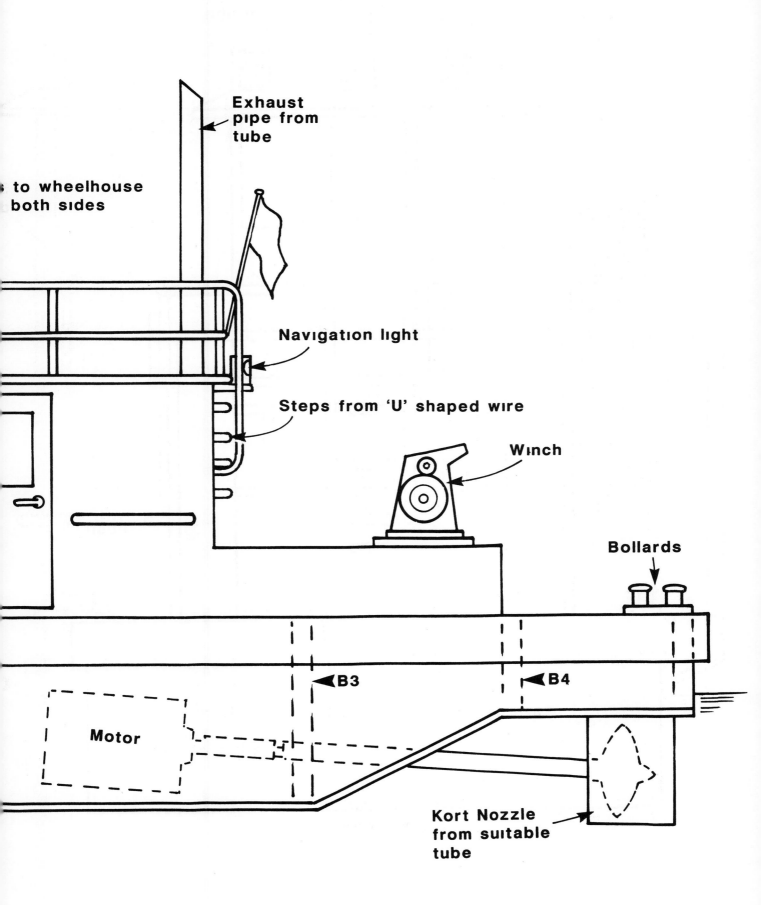

Exhaust pipe from tube

to wheelhouse both sides

Navigation light

Steps from 'U' shaped wire

Winch

Bollards

◄B3

◄B4

Motor

Kort Nozzle from suitable tube

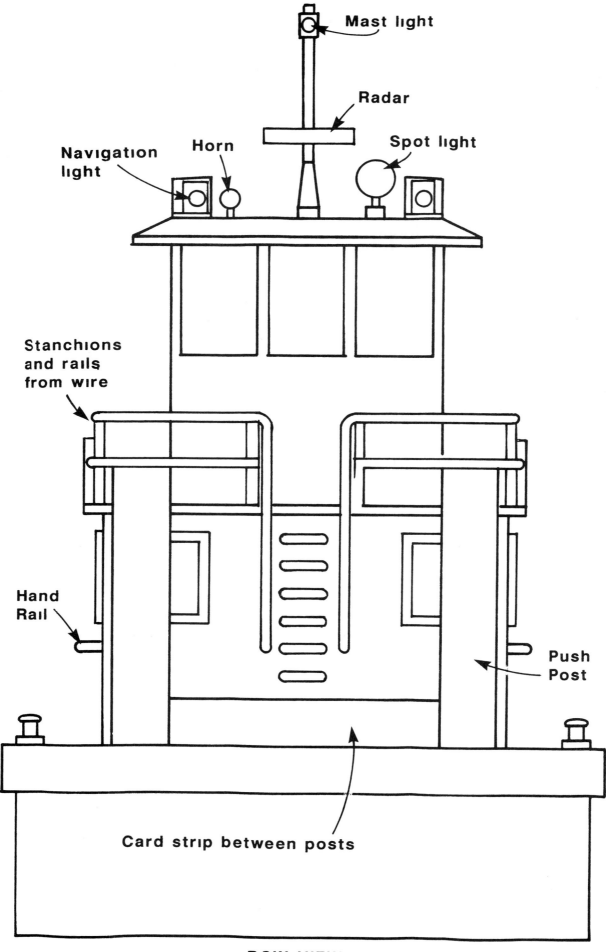

Mast light

Radar

Spot light

Navigation
light

Horn

Stanchions
and rails
from wire

Hand
Rail

Push
Post

Card strip between posts

BOW VIEW

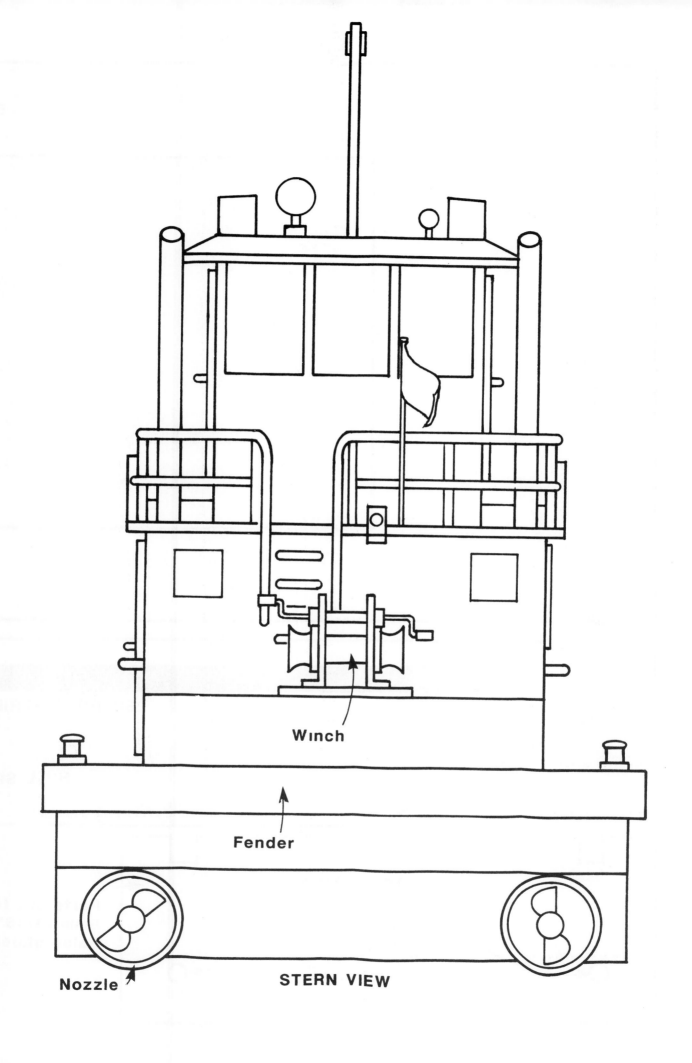

Winch

Fender

Nozzle

STERN VIEW

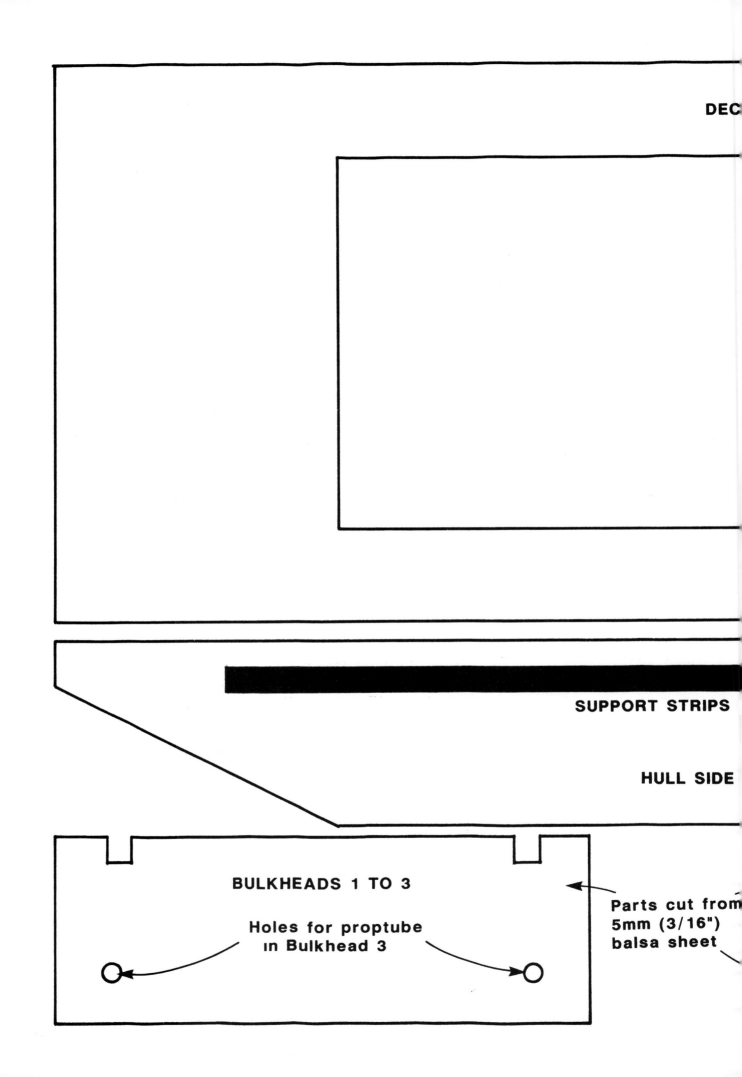

DEC

SUPPORT STRIPS

HULL SIDE

BULKHEADS 1 TO 3

Holes for proptube
in Bulkhead 3

Parts cut from
5mm (3/16")
balsa sheet

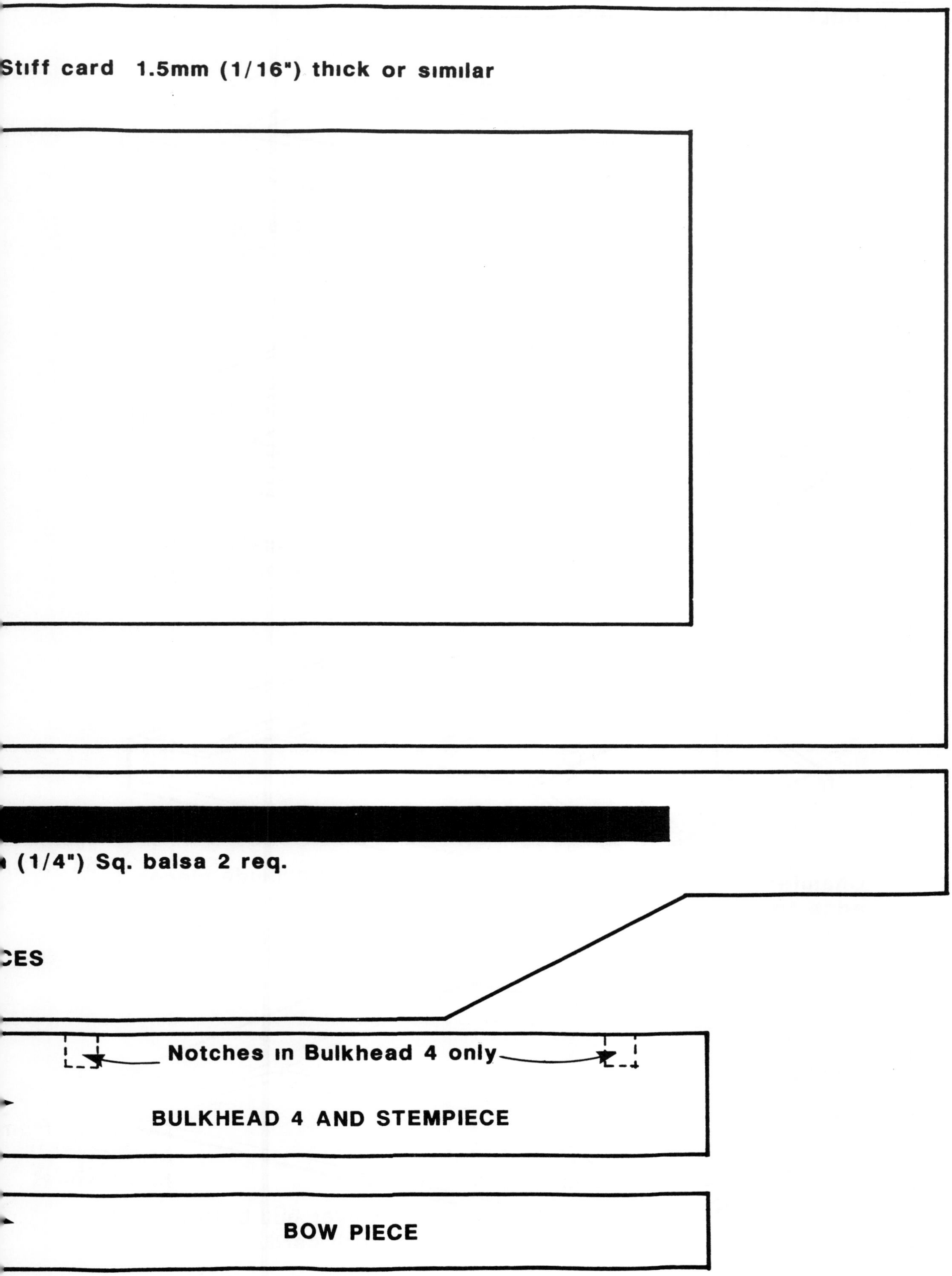

Stiff card 1.5mm (1/16") thick or similar

(1/4") Sq. balsa 2 req.

CES

Notches in Bulkhead 4 only

BULKHEAD 4 AND STEMPIECE

BOW PIECE

HULL BUILDING SEQUENCE
NOTE Hull is built inverted.

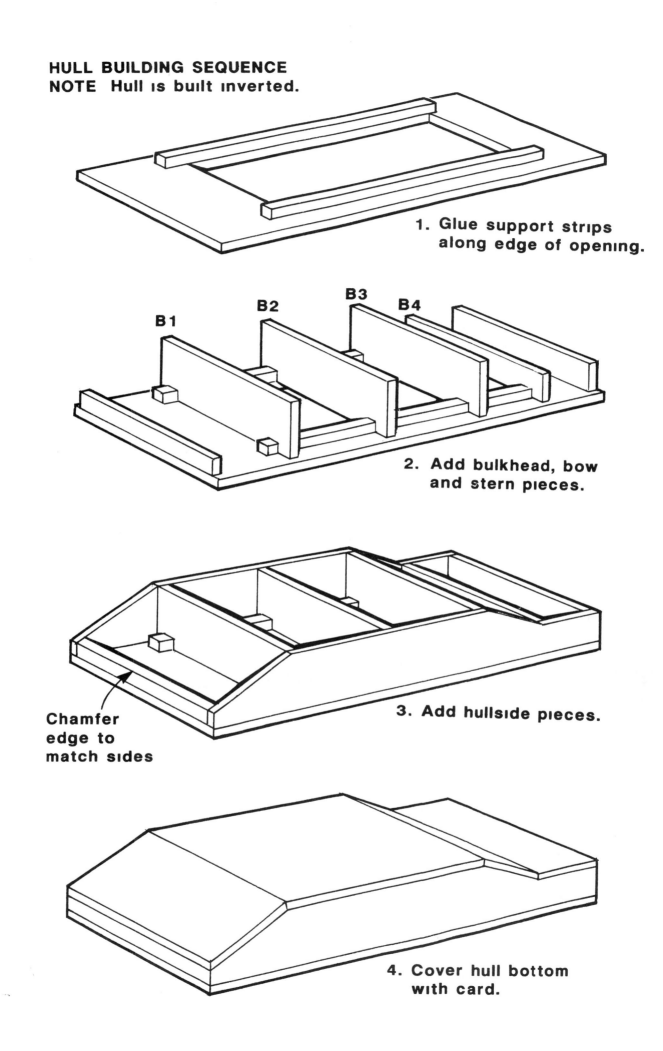

1. Glue support strips along edge of opening.

B1 **B2** **B3** **B4**

2. Add bulkhead, bow and stern pieces.

Chamfer edge to match sides

3. Add hullside pieces.

4. Cover hull bottom with card.

TYPICAL CROSS-SECTION
(Not to scale)

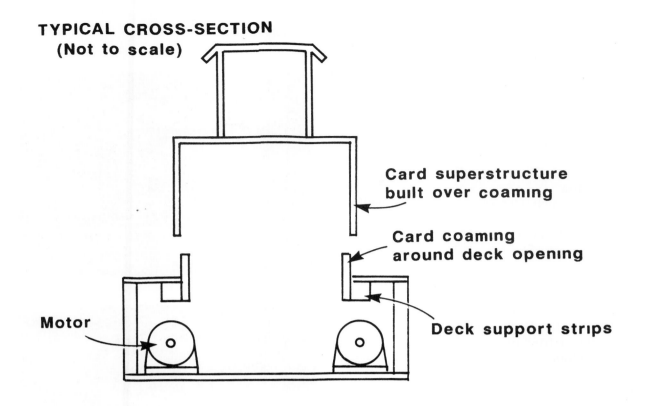

Card superstructure built over coaming

Card coaming around deck opening

Deck support strips

Motor

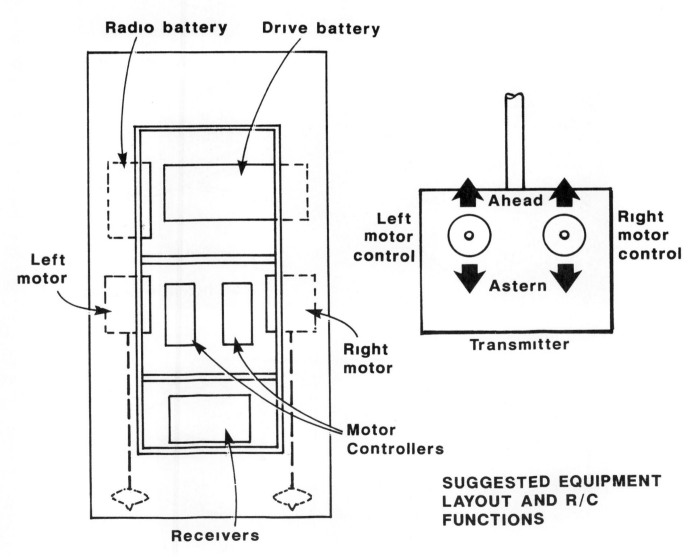

Radio battery

Drive battery

Left motor

Right motor

Motor Controllers

Receivers

Left motor control

Ahead

Astern

Right motor control

Transmitter

SUGGESTED EQUIPMENT LAYOUT AND R/C FUNCTIONS

NB MAKE SURE NOTHING CAN MOVE WHILST SAILING

Basic materials

- One sheet $\frac{3}{16} \times 4$ inch (5×100 millimetre) balsa
- Card $\frac{1}{16}$ inch (1.5 millimetre) thick or plywood
- One strip $\frac{1}{4}$ inch (6 millimetre) square balsa
- Two 3 inch (80 millimetre) long propeller shafts and tubes
- Two Mabuchi-style 360 or 385 motors

Colour scheme

Hull	brick red
Deck	grey
Superstructure	red
Rubbing strips	black

Battery

4–5 nicad cells of 1.2 to 2 Ah capacity

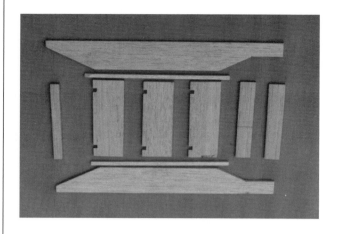

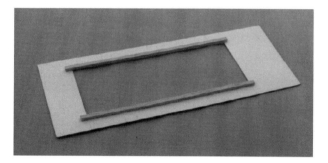

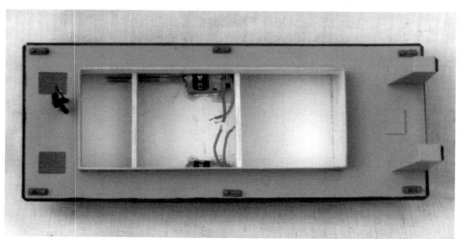

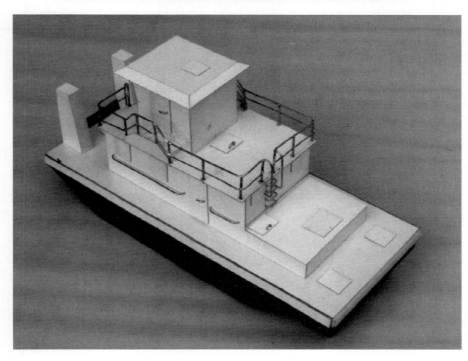

ATCH

During the Vietnam War the US forces made much use of the river system to move troops and weapons. Many landing craft were used, often modified with the addition of armour and guns. This model is based on such a craft which was further altered to support helicopter operations with a landing pad.

The impetus for building this model came when a suitable 1/48 scale helicopter kit was found. This, along with suitable figures and equipment, allows you to build something more akin a military diorama than a working R/C model. Like the previous model, it is intended for twin independently controlled motors but conventional rudders could be used.

HELICOPTER FROM SUITABLE 1/48"KIT
(BELL UH-1C HUEY SHOWN)

WATER LINE
NOTE-BOWS HIGHER THAN STERN.

ARMOURED TROOP CARRIER WITH HELICOPTER PAD. 1/48 SCALE
FOR TWO CHANNEL RADIO CONTROL

COLOUR SCHEME - OVERALL 'DIRTY GREY-GREEN'

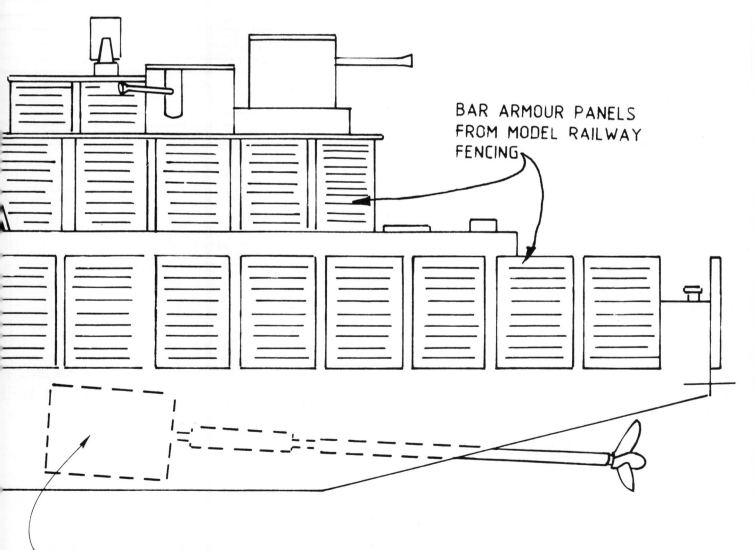

BAR ARMOUR PANELS
FROM MODEL RAILWAY
FENCING

PROPULSION PROVIDED BY TWO
INDEPENDENTLY CONTROLLED MOTORS

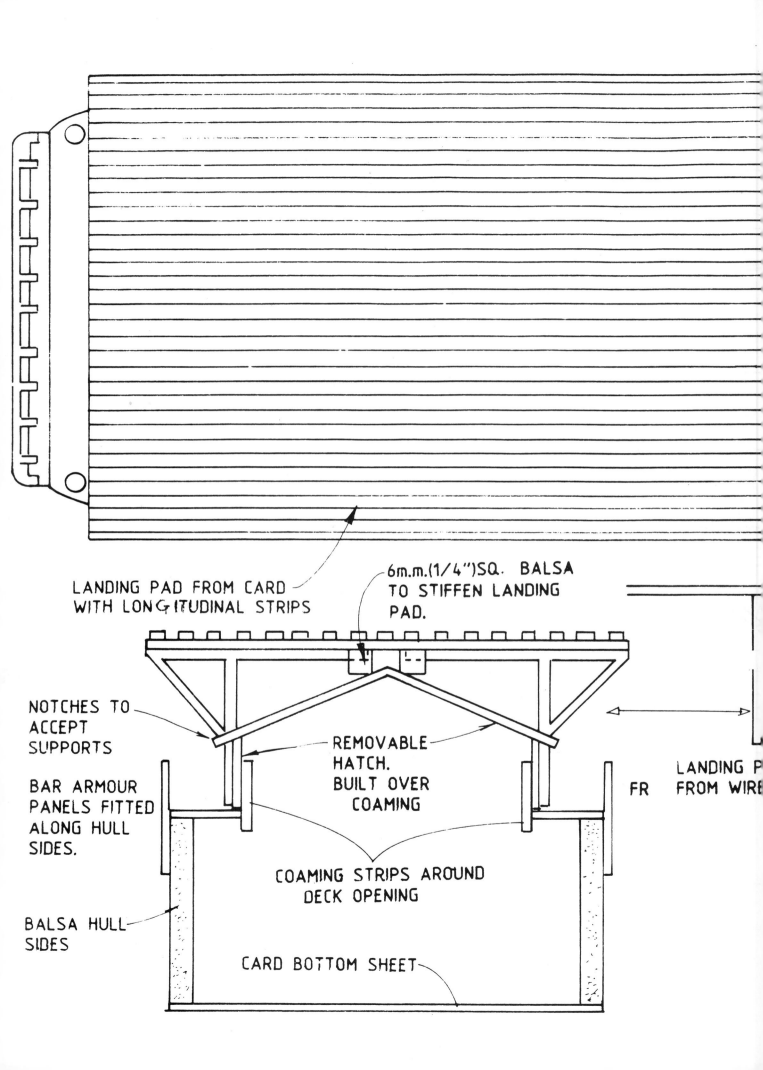

LANDING PAD FROM CARD
WITH LONGITUDINAL STRIPS

6m.m.(1/4")SQ. BALSA
TO STIFFEN LANDING
PAD.

NOTCHES TO
ACCEPT
SUPPORTS

BAR ARMOUR
PANELS FITTED
ALONG HULL
SIDES.

REMOVABLE
HATCH.
BUILT OVER
COAMING

LANDING P
FROM WIRE

FR

BALSA HULL
SIDES

COAMING STRIPS AROUND
DECK OPENING

CARD BOTTOM SHEET

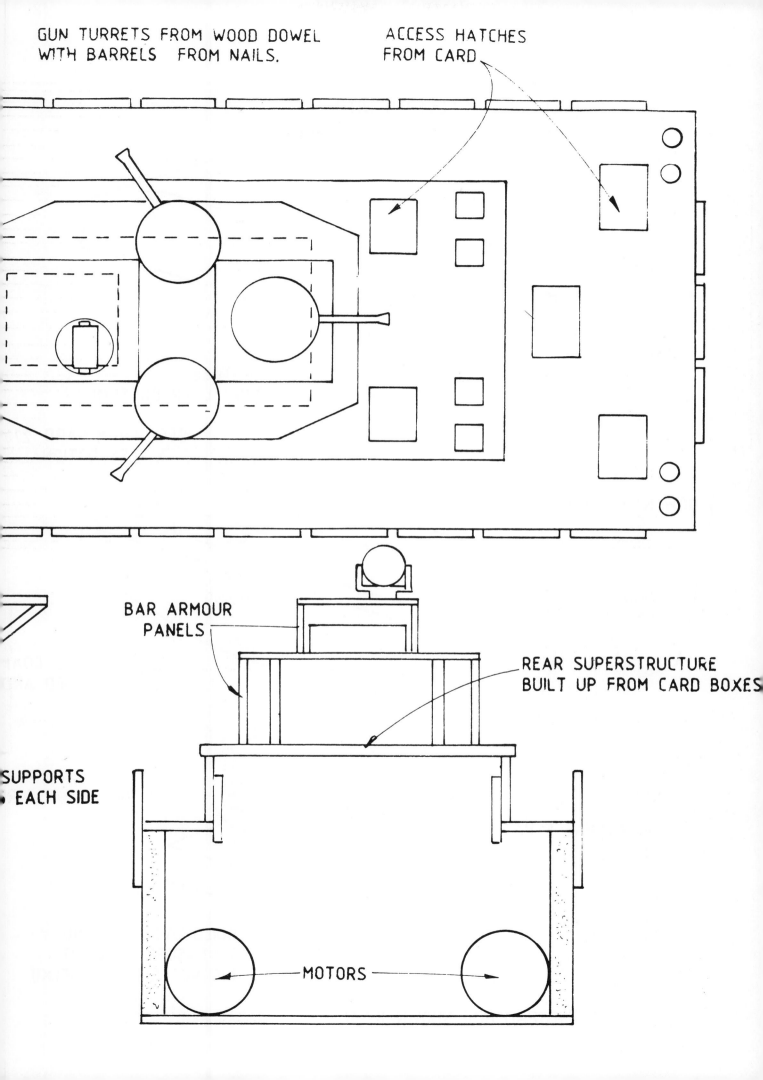

GUN TURRETS FROM WOOD DOWEL
WITH BARRELS FROM NAILS.

ACCESS HATCHES
FROM CARD

BAR ARMOUR
PANELS

REAR SUPERSTRUCTURE
BUILT UP FROM CARD BOXES

SUPPORTS
EACH SIDE

MOTORS

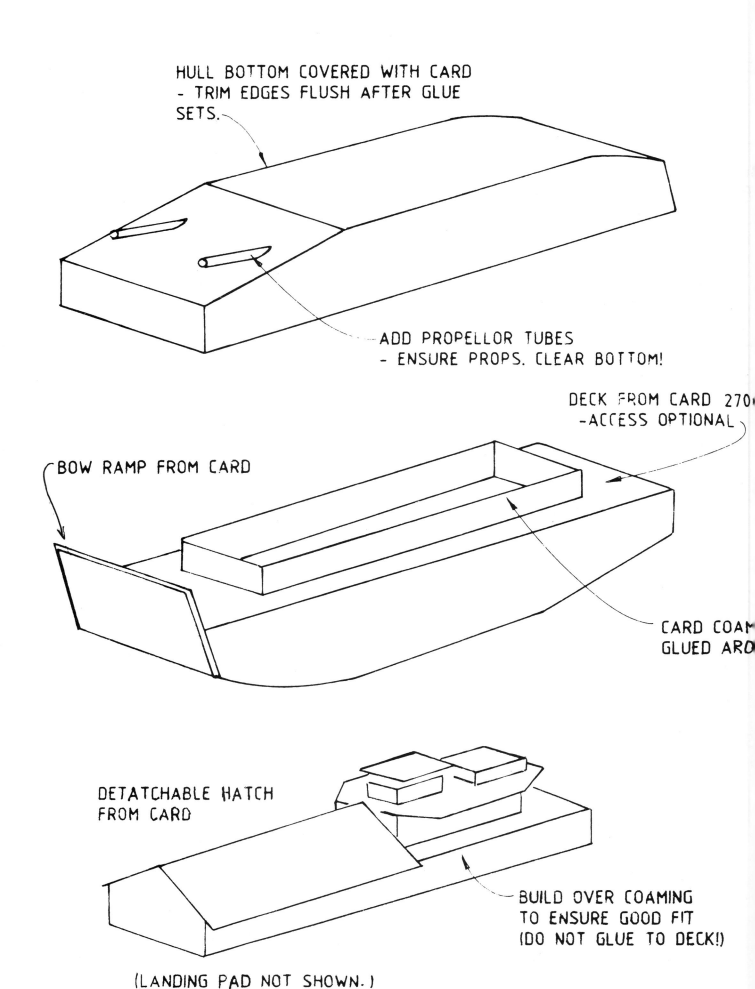

HULL BOTTOM COVERED WITH CARD
- TRIM EDGES FLUSH AFTER GLUE
SETS.

ADD PROPELLOR TUBES
- ENSURE PROPS. CLEAR BOTTOM!

DECK FROM CARD 270
-ACCESS OPTIONAL

BOW RAMP FROM CARD

CARD COAM
GLUED ARO

DETATCHABLE HATCH
FROM CARD

BUILD OVER COAMING
TO ENSURE GOOD FIT
(DO NOT GLUE TO DECK!)

(LANDING PAD NOT SHOWN.)

FRAME FROM WIRE
EPOXIED TO RAMP.

OW RAMP
ROM THICK CARD

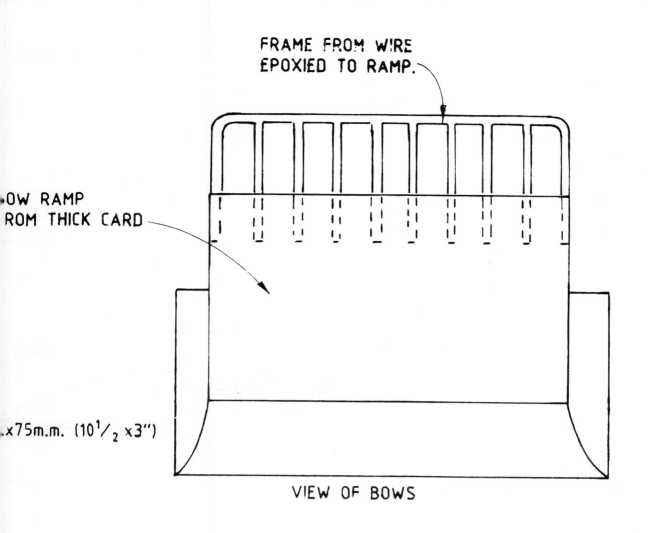

x75m.m. (10½ x3")

VIEW OF BOWS

DRIVE
BATTERY PACK

MOTOR   COUPLING   RECEIVER

DECK

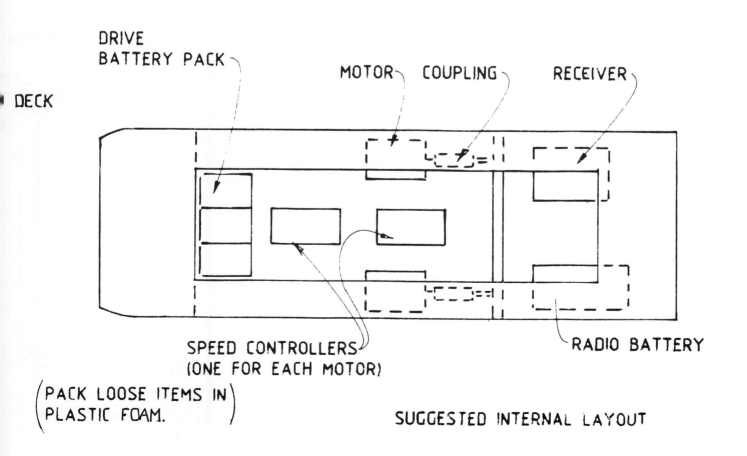

SPEED CONTROLLERS
(ONE FOR EACH MOTOR)

RADIO BATTERY

(PACK LOOSE ITEMS IN
 PLASTIC FOAM.)

SUGGESTED INTERNAL LAYOUT

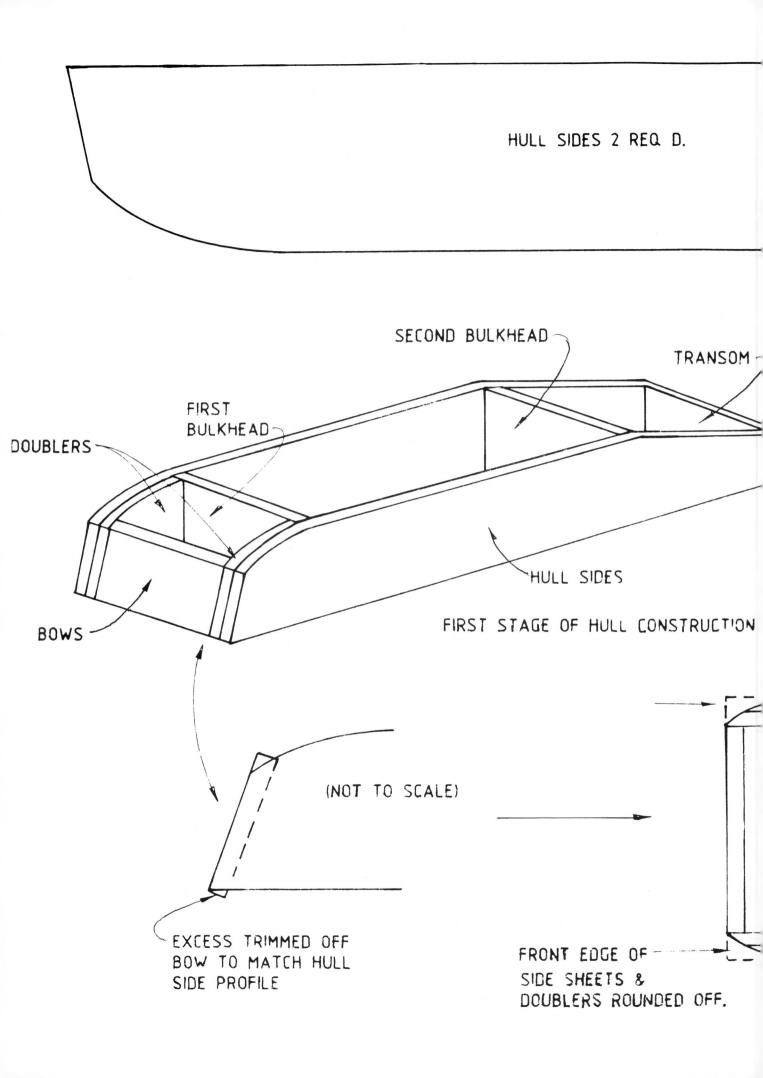

HULL SIDES 2 REQ D.

SECOND BULKHEAD

TRANSOM

FIRST
BULKHEAD

DOUBLERS

HULL SIDES

FIRST STAGE OF HULL CONSTRUCTION

BOWS

(NOT TO SCALE)

EXCESS TRIMMED OFF
BOW TO MATCH HULL
SIDE PROFILE

FRONT EDGE OF
SIDE SHEETS &
DOUBLERS ROUNDED OFF.

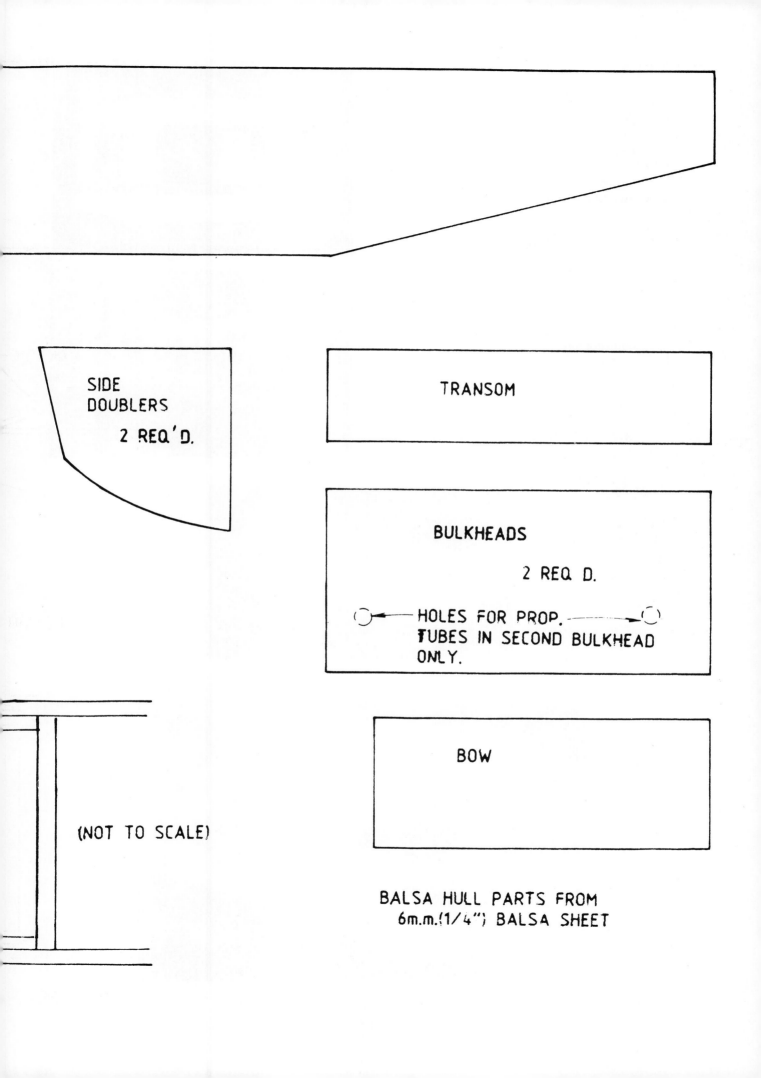

SIDE
DOUBLERS

2 REQ'D.

TRANSOM

BULKHEADS

2 REQ D.

HOLES FOR PROP.
TUBES IN SECOND BULKHEAD
ONLY.

BOW

(NOT TO SCALE)

BALSA HULL PARTS FROM
6m.m.(1/4") BALSA SHEET

Basic materials

- One sheet ½ × 4 inch (6 × 100 millime-tre) balsa
- Card sheet 1–1.5mm thick
- Two 3 inch (80 millimetre) long propeller shafts and tubes
- Two Mabuchi-style 280 or 385 motors

Colour scheme

Overall a dirty grey–green colour

Hull below waterline green – weed stained

Landing pad white
markings

Battery

3–4 nicad cells of 1.2 to 2 Ah capacity.

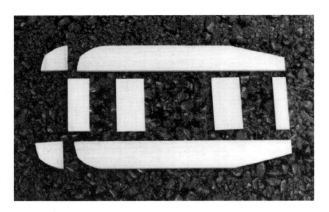

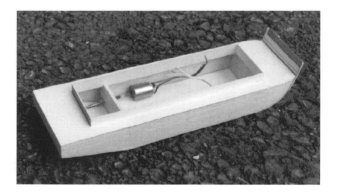

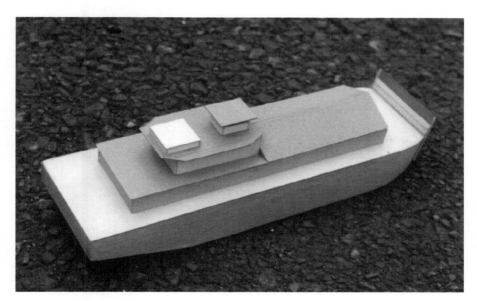

GUARDIAN

Catamaran twin hull type of vessels are not new but recently they have become popular for small patrol ships. The twin hulls offer excellent stability and a large deck area without excessive displacement. A catamaran design creates a few extra design problems for the modeller but *Guardian* proved to be relatively easy to build and very safe to sail.

The large deck area cried out to be used as a helicopter landing pad. A kit based upon a US Navy type was obtained and the attractive red, white and blue US Coast Guard colour scheme seemed only natural. Like the previous models, *Guardian* was designed for independent control of twin motors. Twin rudders could be added aft of the propellers if desired.

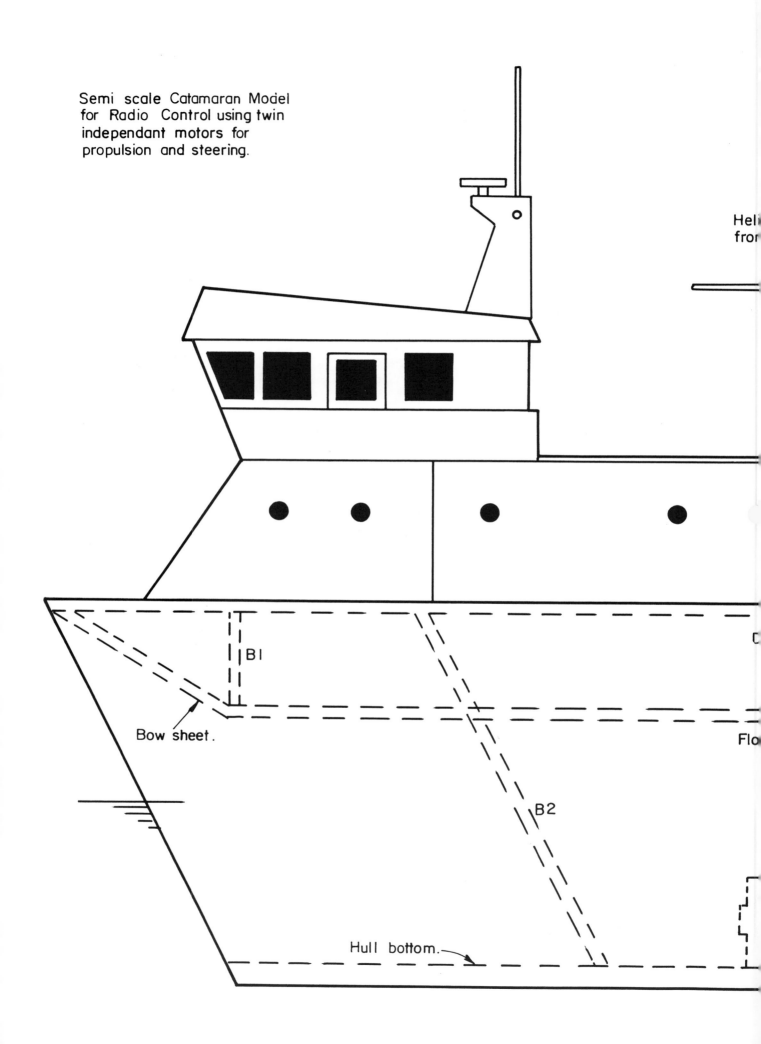

Semi scale Catamaran Model
for Radio Control using twin
independant motors for
propulsion and steering.

Heli
fror

B1

Bow sheet.

Flo

B2

Hull bottom.

Suggested Equipment Layout.

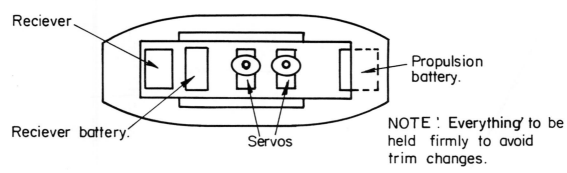

Reciever

Reciever battery.

Servos

Propulsion battery.

NOTE : Everything' to be held firmly to avoid trim changes.

er – Scratch built or
table kit – KAMAN SH – 2F Seasprite shown.

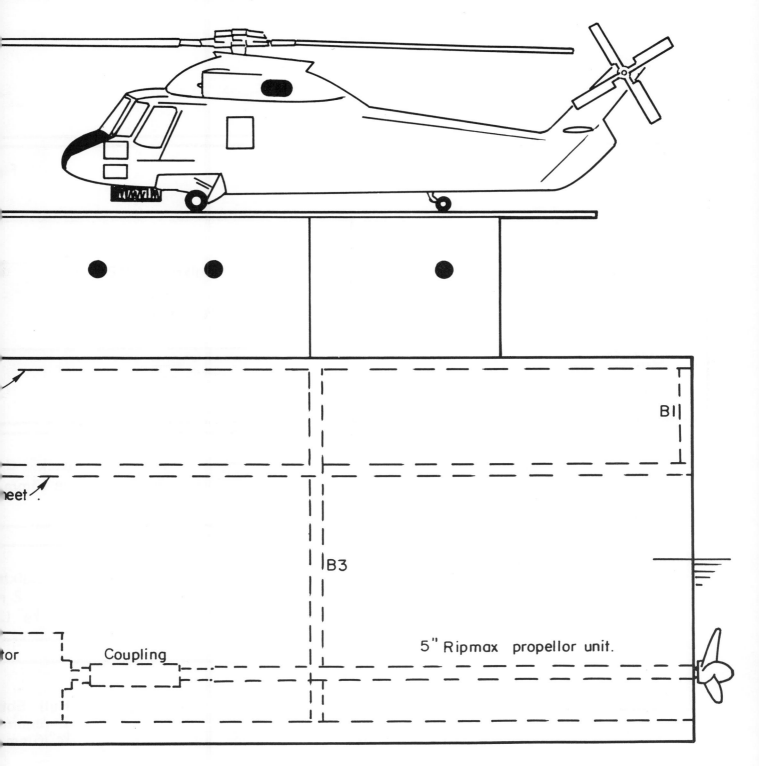

B1

eet .

B3

tor

Coupling

5" Ripmax propellor unit.

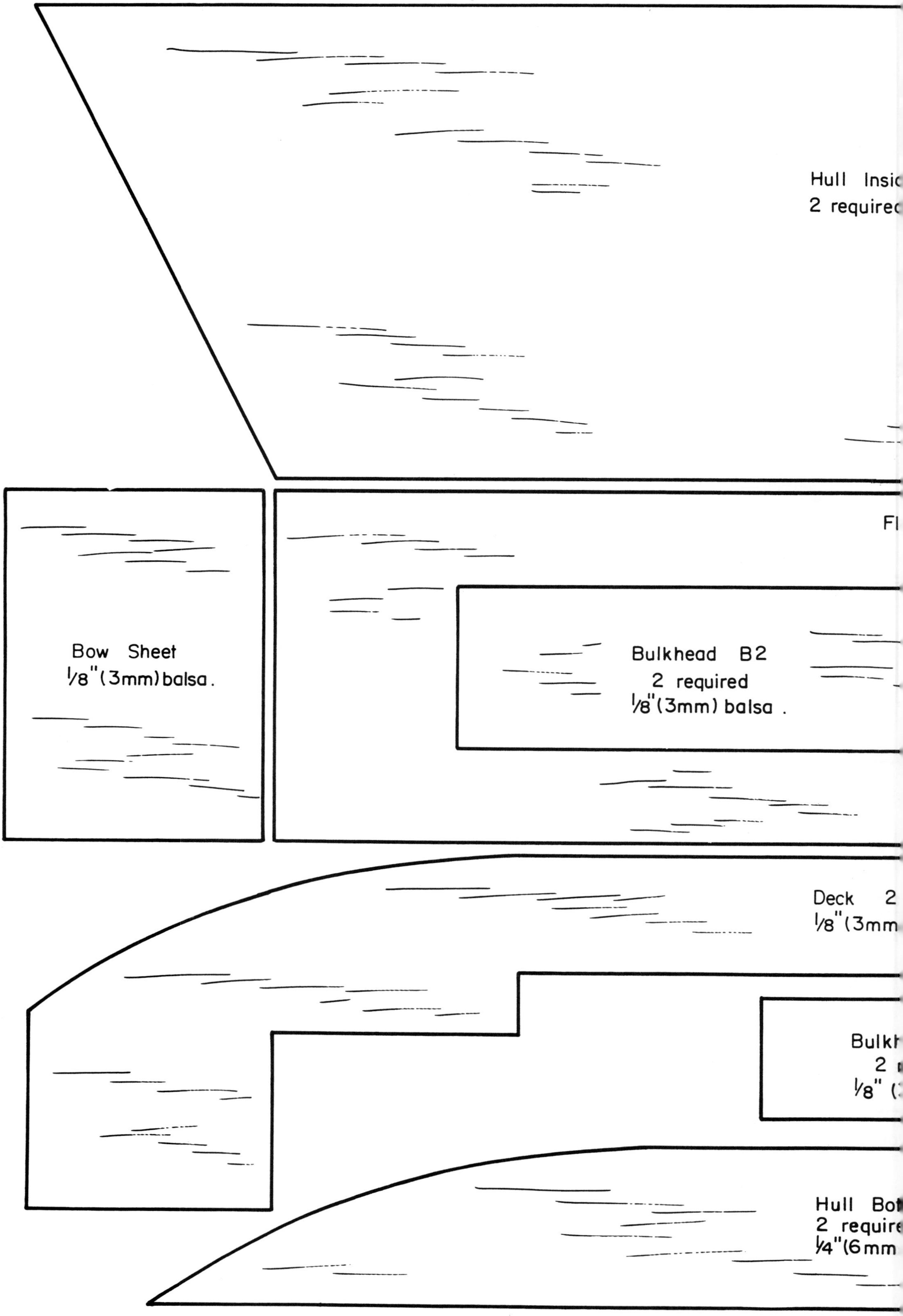

Hull Insid
2 required

Bow Sheet
1/8"(3mm) balsa.

Fl

Bulkhead B2
2 required
1/8"(3mm) balsa.

Deck   2
1/8"(3mm

Bulkh
2
1/8" (3

Hull Bot
2 require
1/4"(6mm

eet
(3mm) balsa

Sheet ⅛"(3mm) balsa.

Bulkhead   B3
2 required
⅛"(3mm)balsa.

ed
a.

BI.
ed
balsa.

a.

CONSTRUCTION SEQUENCE

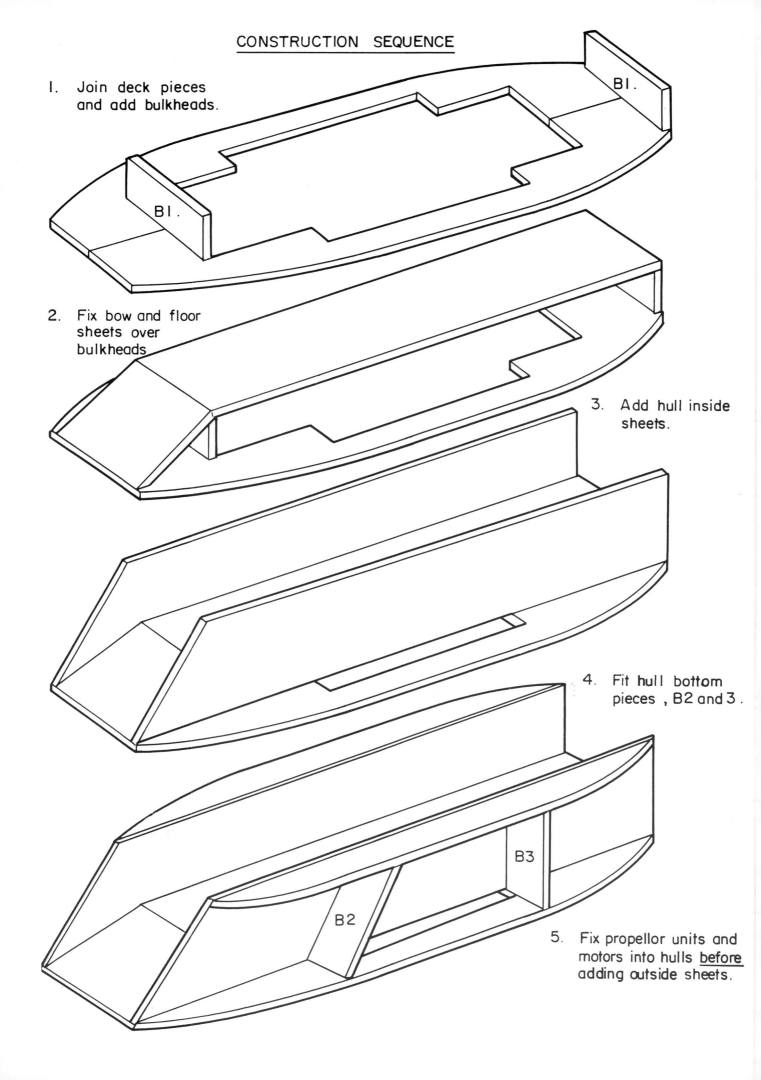

1. Join deck pieces and add bulkheads.

B1.

B1.

2. Fix bow and floor sheets over bulkheads.

3. Add hull inside sheets.

4. Fit hull bottom pieces, B2 and 3.

B3

B2

5. Fix propellor units and motors into hulls **before** adding outside sheets.

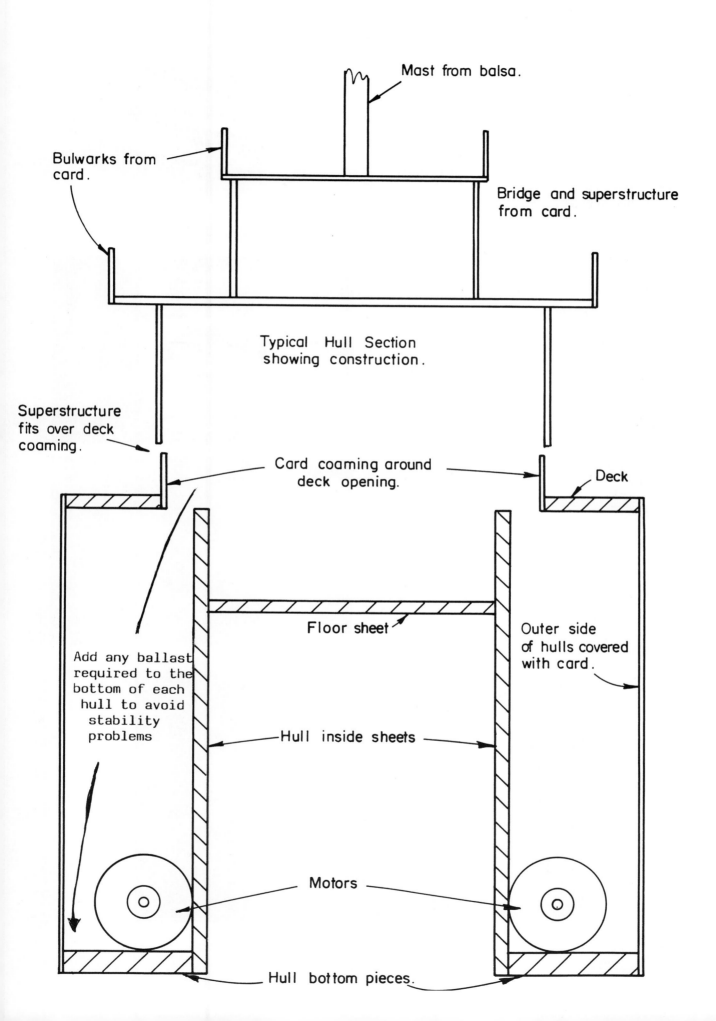

Mast from balsa.

Bulwarks from card.

Bridge and superstructure from card.

Typical Hull Section showing construction.

Superstructure fits over deck coaming.

Card coaming around deck opening.

Deck

Floor sheet

Outer side of hulls covered with card.

Add any ballast required to the bottom of each hull to avoid stability problems

Hull inside sheets

Motors

Hull bottom pieces.

Basic materials

- One sheet ⅛ × 4 inch (3 × 100 millimetre) balsa
- One sheet ⅛ × 3 inch (3 × 75 millimetre) balsa
- One sheet ¼ × 3 inch (6 × 75 millimetre) balsa
- Card sheet 1mm thick
- Two 5 inch (125 millimetre) long propeller shafts and tubes
- Two Mabuchi-style 280 or 360 motors

Colour scheme

Hull	below waterline red above waterline white
Decks	matt green
Superstructure	white
Waterline stripe	black self-adhesive tape
Hull side stripes	red and blue self-adhesive tape

Battery

2–4 nicad cells of 1.2 Ah capacity to give a lively performance without handling difficulties.

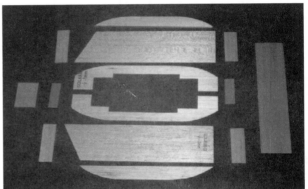

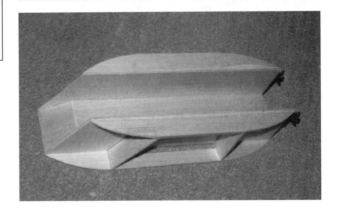

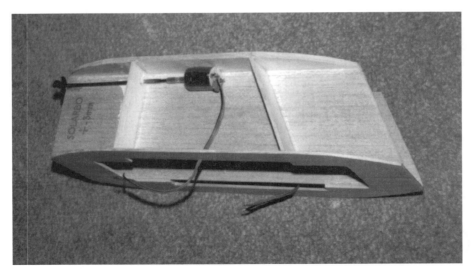

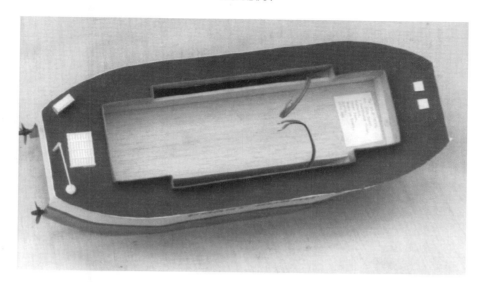

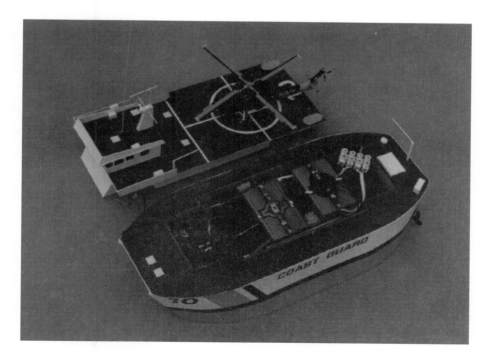

ELECTRON

This model was intended to show that small models can be fast as well as economical to build. Using a standard '540' type motor and 6 nicads it has the speed and stability to race with most commercial kits. It is not suitable for a first R/C model but makes an excellent diversion for the reasonably experienced modeller.

A simple heavy duty ON–OFF switch operated by a servo is ideal for this model. The resistive boards used in the other models are *not suitable*. Only use this model on large safe waters and respect other people's models!

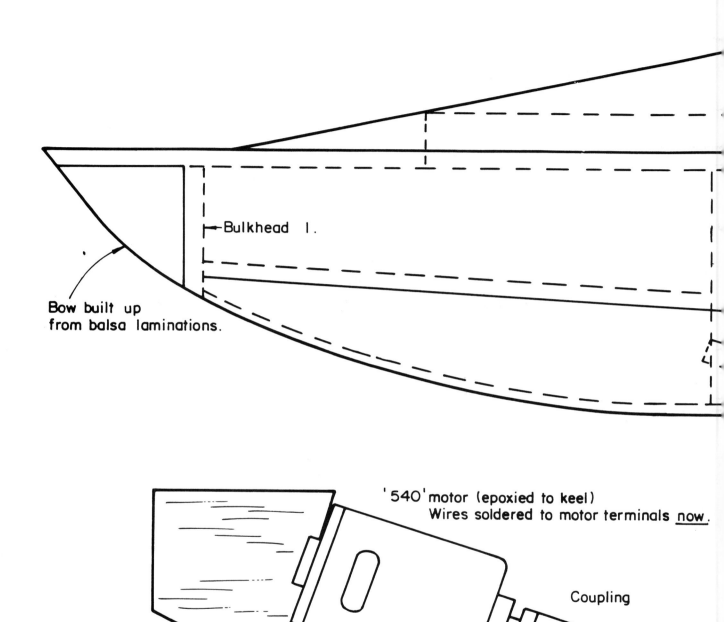

Bulkhead I.

Bow built up
from balsa laminations.

'540' motor (epoxied to keel)
Wires soldered to motor terminals <u>now</u>.

Coupling

'Keel' before building
into the hull.

5"(1'

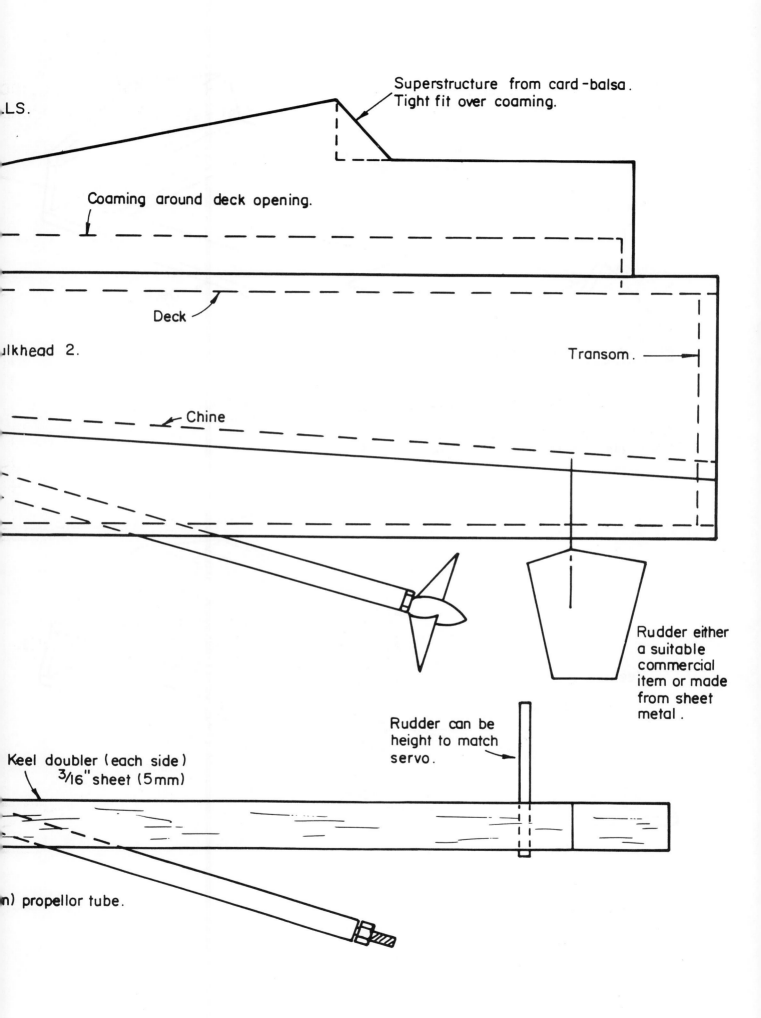

Superstructure from card-balsa.
Tight fit over coaming.

.LS.

Coaming around deck opening.

Deck

ulkhead 2.

Transom.

Chine

Rudder either a suitable commercial item or made from sheet metal.

Rudder can be height to match servo.

Keel doubler (each side) 3/16" sheet (5mm)

n) propellor tube.

HULL CONSTRUCTION

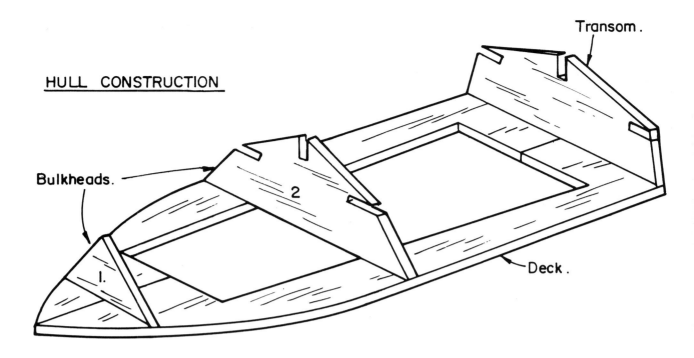

1) Join two deck pieces – keep flat untill dry.

2) Add bulkheads and transom – keep square.

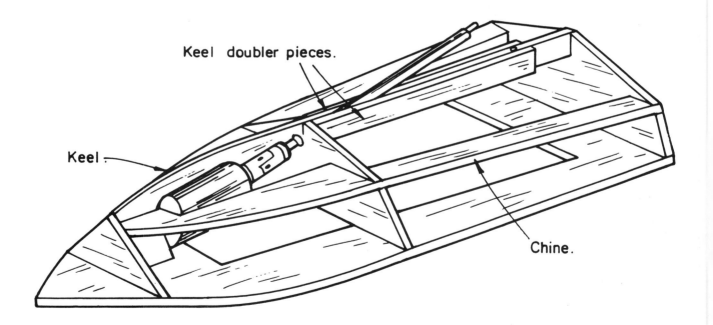

3) Add keel and chine pieces.

4) Epoxy motor to chine pieces.

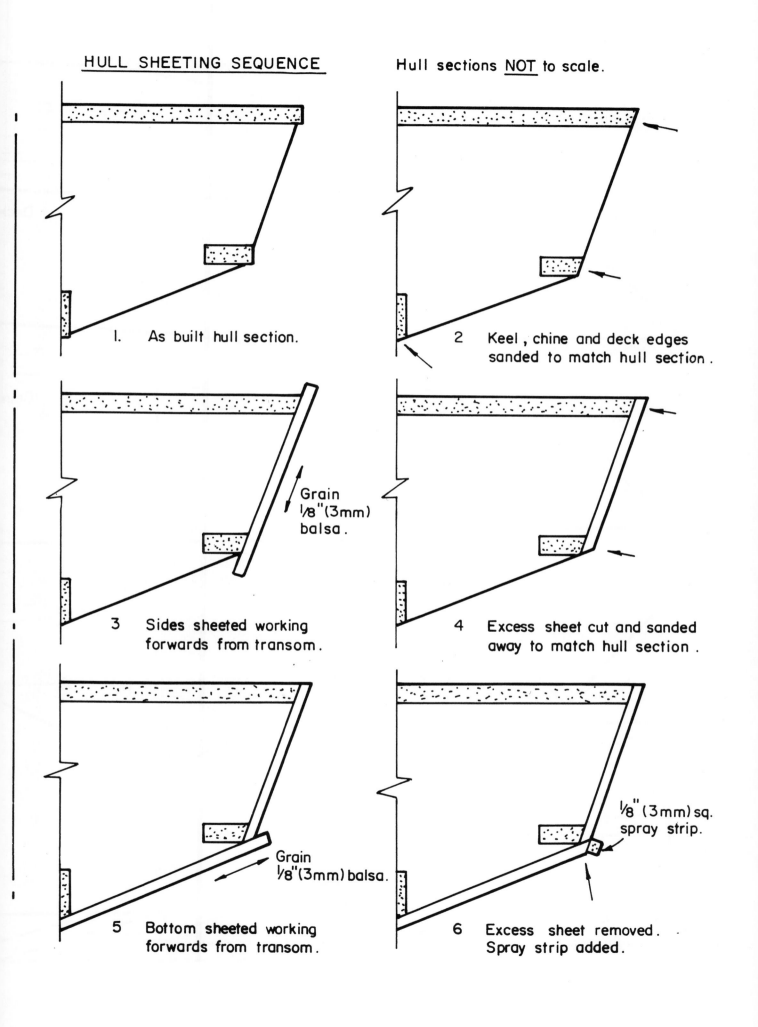

HULL SHEETING SEQUENCE

Hull sections NOT to scale.

1. As built hull section.

2 Keel, chine and deck edges sanded to match hull section.

3 Sides sheeted working forwards from transom.

Grain 1/8"(3mm) balsa.

4 Excess sheet cut and sanded away to match hull section.

5 Bottom sheeted working forwards from transom.

Grain 1/8"(3mm) balsa.

6 Excess sheet removed. Spray strip added.

1/8" (3mm) sq. spray strip.

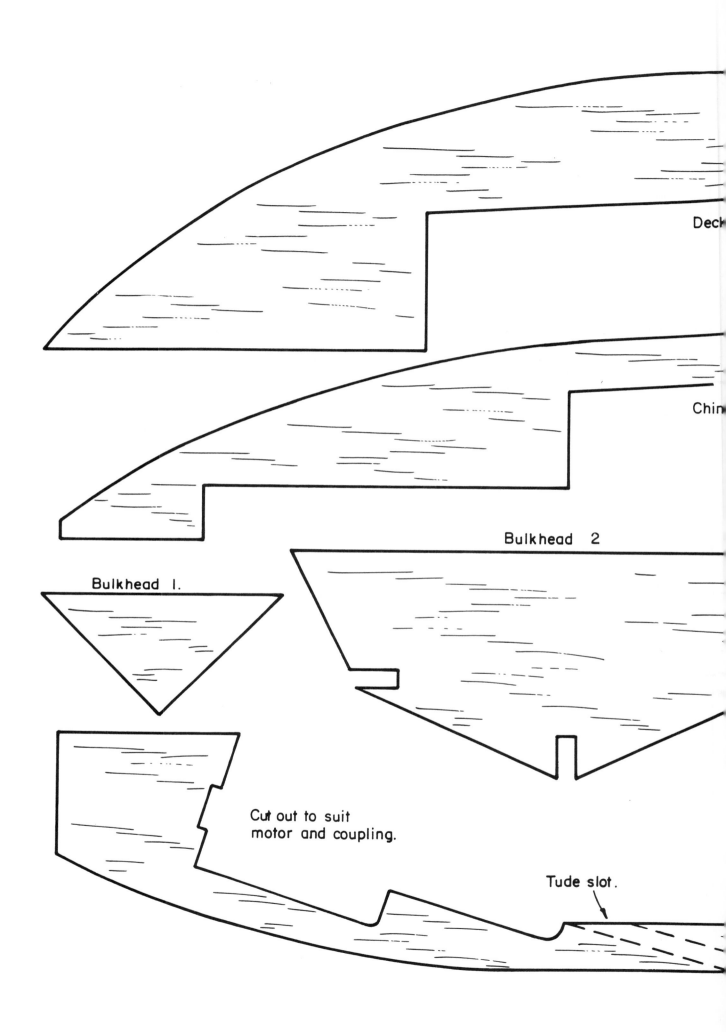

Deck

Chine

Bulkhead 2

Bulkhead 1.

Cut out to suit
motor and coupling.

Tube slot.

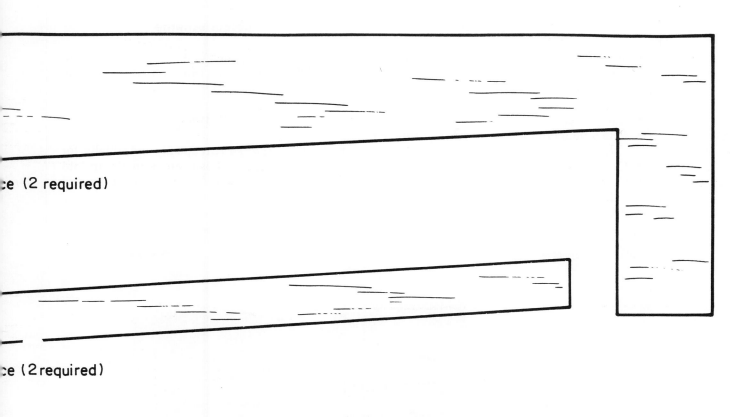

ce (2 required)

ce (2 required)

Balsa parts from ³⁄16″(5mm) sheet.

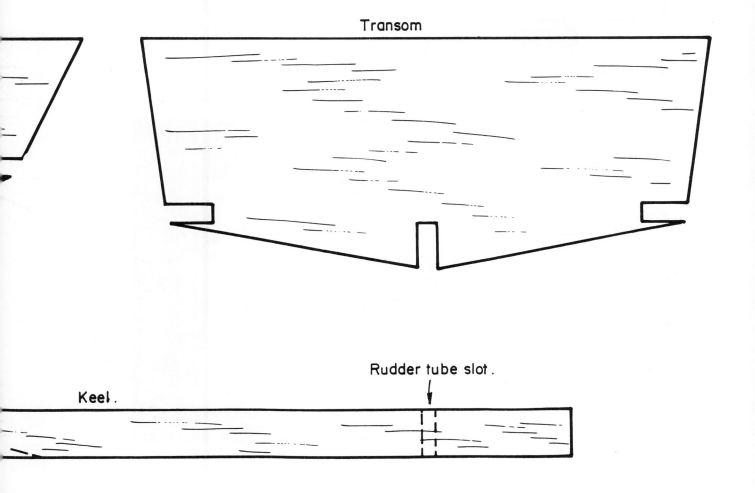

Transom

Rudder tube slot.

Keel.

Basic materials

- Two sheets ³⁄₁₆ × 3 inch (5 × 75 millimetre) balsa
- Two sheets ⅛ × 3 inch (3 × 75 millimetre) balsa
- Card sheet 1mm thick
- One 5 inch (125 millimetre) long propeller shaft and tube
- One Mabuchi-style 540 motor
- Coupling to match motor and propeller shafts
- 30mm diameter racing propeller

Colour scheme

Anything bright which makes the model easy to see! Trim can be added from self-adhesive tape.

Battery

6 nicads of 1.2 to 1.7 Ah capacity and suitable for rapid discharging. These can be made up into two packs of 3 cells to fit either side of the keel behind bulkhead 3.

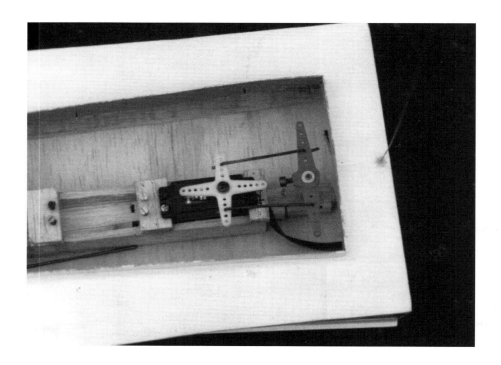

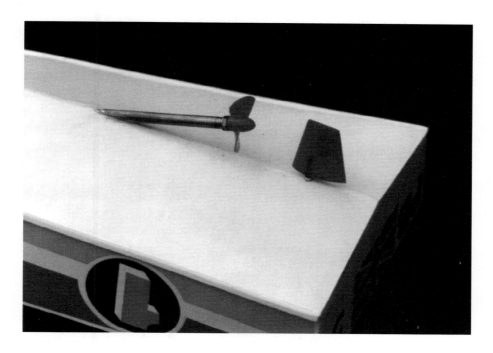

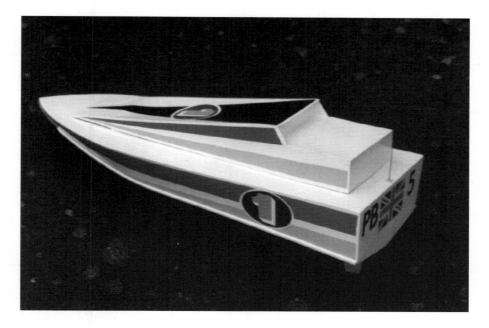